# Praise for *I Remember You*

*I Remember You* is a delight to read. The characters in Elaine's memoir come alive on the page. I can see and hear them all. I'm also treated to a front row seat to Elaine's development as the main character in her life story as she deftly traces her movement to self-acceptance, healing, and joy. Always joy

—*Dr. Michael Schiefelbein*, teacher, writer, and minister

If you were to create a word cloud for Elaine Blanchard's new book, the largest and most prominent words would be *courageous, trauma, commitment, survivor.* By sharing her trauma, Elaine enables us to share our own. There are some things we can't talk about, but talk about them, we must in order to heal. *I Remember You* gives us the language to do just that. In *I Remember You*, Elaine Blanchard reminds us that our secrets keep us sick. Read this book, and let the healing begin.

—*Jack Richbourg*, author, lawyer, activist

"In Elaine Blanchard's heartfelt memoir, she reminds us that our ailments and our best selves together can activate us toward change. It is a moving portrait of the somewhat small and also significant effect we have on each other and the larger world around us.

—*David Prete*, author of *August and Then Some*

Elaine's story is about the majesty of soul—hers and ours—in its relentless reach for life, faith, and all that is good—a majesty revealed most powerfully in our journey through wounds. *I Remember You: The Making of an Activist* is a story of spiritual growth and survival, a sermon of reckoning, showing how brokenness, illness, and addiction can become thresholds to compassion, creativity, and advocacy. As a playwright, actor, and pastor, Elaine discovered healing for herself while opening paths of renewal for others, teaching that when we share our stories, they can deepen the spirit and lift us all. At the heart of her riveting testament lies a long-hidden revelation, where a deep childhood guilt is transformed into grace, releasing her to claim her voice with new strength and step fully into the work of justice.

—Sarah Brown: playwright, Director and Professor of Performance at
the University of Memphis

In *I Remember You: The Making of An Activist,* Elaine Blanchard tells the story of her life, filled with fresh starts, fierce loves, fiery conversations—and finally, peace and joy. Elaine's story of ditching shame and secrets to find healing and hope will resonate with readers who yearn to find meaning in their own life stories. I couldn't put it down!

—*Rochelle Melander*, author of *Mightier Than the Sword: Rebels,
Reformers, and Revolutionaries Who Changed the World through Writing*

*There is no greater agony*
*than bearing an untold story.*

Zora Neale Hurston

# I Remember You

## The Making of an Activist

ELAINE BLANCHARD

Bohannon Hall Press

Printed in the United States of America
First Edition

Cover Design by Bohannon Hall Press

Library of Congress Control Number: 2025914011

Publisher's Cataloging-in-Publication Data

Blanchard, Elaine, 1952-
    I Remember You: The Making of an Activist / by Elaine Blanchard.
    Niceville, FL: Bohannon Hall Press, 2025.
    240 p.: 18 cm.
    First edition.

1. Blanchard, Elaine, 1952- —Personal Memoirs. I. Biography &
Autobiography —Personal Memoirs. II. Biography & Autobiography—
Social Activists. III. Biography & Autobiography—Women.

E184.37.B53 I1 2025                                    2025914011

ISBN 978-1-962995-11-5 softcover)

Published by Bohannon Hall Press

**This book contains mature themes and may not be suitable for all readers.
Incidents of sexual abuse, violence and racial epithets are depicted.**

*To Abram*

*who has brought such great joy into our lives*

# Table of Contents

# PREFACE

It is the week before the 2024 presidential election and I am the pastor of a small, courageous and loving congregation in Union City, Tennessee. My people have been nervous about the election and what its outcome might be. I spoke directly to that fear on Sunday, the Sunday before we all voted on Tuesday. I told my congregation about *hesed* the Hebrew word for God's steadfast love, God's covenant love. Rev. Frank Thomas says, "In the Hebrew scriptures *hesed* was a principle. But in the New Testament *hesed* is a person by the name of Jesus the Christ." Trusting in God's *hesed* is the entry way to hope. Once we truly give ourselves over to God's unchanging and undimming love, we realize all will be well and all manner of things will be well, to quote Julian of Norwich. Truly we are living in dark times. The election won't satisfy much of the nation. But I trust the goodness in this world to be obvious at all times because the love of God lives in so many of us. That light will shine among us because we have given ourselves to something other than, bigger than, ourselves. We belong to the *hesed* of God.

I am reminded of the people of Le Chambon, that little French village with its Lutheran Church. Those ordinary citizens risked their own safety, their own lives, to save Jewish refugees from the Vichy Government and the Nazis. They rescued 5000 Jews, helping them to hide and also helping some to cross the border into Switzerland. Ordinary people who let the light shine through them. Every home and barn became a sanctuary. The Jewish children were enrolled in the public schools. It's amazing how the love of God can move us into action.

I couldn't tell this story without including other people. My life has been a series of relationships, as all lives tend to be. I have changed the names of many characters to provide privacy for those who might not want to be included in my story. I have been damaged along the way and those who have damaged me are part of my story as well as those who have supported my healing. It is not my intent to disparage anyone but simply to share my own life experiences. I have come out strong in the broken places and that is the purpose of my sharing these life stories. Like the Japanese art called Kintsugi, the practice of repairing broken pottery by mending the cracks with lacquer mixed with powdered gold, silver or platinum. Instead of hiding the damage, Kintsugi embraces flaws as part of the object's history. I have accepted what life has given me.

I am fortunate to be loved by my beautiful wife, Anna, who has put up with more than most would have as I have bumped around from job to job for years, trying to find a place that can hold on to me. She has been a rock. Together, over the last twenty-five years, Anna and I have built a home that satisfies us. We are surrounded by an abundance of good friends and family. I can look back from this safe place and give thanks for all that my life has been and will be.

# CHAPTER I

## MY FIRST THERAPIST

It was 1978, and I entered therapy for the first time. I had a daughter who was two years old, and I wanted to be a good mother for her. My own mother had been depressed early in my life. I was feeling unhappy and I wanted to be more joyful so I went into therapy, hoping that would help me avoid the mistakes my mother had made. I had a disturbing memory, a memory about a black boy in the field across the avenue from our house, a memory from my childhood in Gainesville, Florida. If the memory was real, then my family was not at all who I had always believed them to be. I believed they were good people, and good people wouldn't do the things that were coming up in my memory.

Daniel, a young white man just out of graduate school, was a licensed clinical psychologist. He worked at the Community

Mental Health Center and was affordable. He wasn't handsome like a movie star, but he was neat looking, and I imagined his mother being very proud of him and his accomplishments. His curly brown hair seemed unmanageable, and it looked as if he had long ago given up the fight. He pushed a strand away from his eyes as he held a pen and paper and made notes. I sat in a recliner and talked about my troubled marriage, and my loneliness. I was twenty-six, and I was just realizing the possibility that life can be planned rather than being hurled from one thing to another. Having a child settled me and caused me to reflect. I had already earned my associate degree in nursing and was working as a registered nurse at Jackson General Hospital in Tennessee. I was Doug's wife and Jennifer's mother. Week after week, in Daniel's tiny office, I picked through memories of my childhood. I longed to know what had happened to the black boy. "I have this blurry memory of a black boy. He talked with me and then, I think, something happened, maybe something awful. But that's the part I can't remember, and it makes me wonder if the memory is real." It seemed to me that, whether the memory was real or not, the boy and I were deeply connected. I wanted to know his name. I wanted to know if he existed or whether I only imagined him.

I was raised in a religious household dominated by my father and three brothers. Eric, Eugene, and Edward were older than me. Eric and Eugene were in middle and high school by the time I was old enough to have memories. They had girlfriends of their own, baseball games that called for our whole family to sit in the bleachers and holler words of encouragement. They had instruments, a trombone and a tuba, to play in the high school band. Edward was one year older than me. When he started kindergarten, I was left at home without a playmate. Daddy was the preacher at First Church of the Nazarene, next door to our house. He was always busy, and Mama was busy helping him. She was his secretary, though unpaid. She also played the piano for worship services. Again, unpaid work. They were focused on church duties, so I found myself looking for fun on my own.

I sat on the front steps of our downtown parsonage, and watched as people parked their cars. I knew everybody who worked downtown… Red was the manager at Kilgore's Feed and Seed. He would put a stool beside a seed barrel that stood on his show room floor, inviting me to run my hands through the seeds, scooping corn and oats, and letting them fall back into the barrel. Harold worked at Lillian's Music Store, the place where Daddy got his music for playing organ at the church and at the funeral home, Chapel of the Chimes. Mr. Chase owned Chase's Home Hardware and Appliances. I had a crush on Mr. Chase. He was tall and handsome. I ran beside him as he walked from his car to the front door of his store.

I told him everything I had done the day before and everything I planned to do that day. He patted me on the head, keeping an arm's length from my sticky face and hands. Mr. Smith owned Smith's Gulf Station on the corner. He was a member of our church and his son, Smitty, was best friends with my oldest brother, Eric. I knew Mr. Smith very well. He had a Tom's Peanut and Candy case in his gas station. I was down there every day with a penny in my hand, hanging on the door of that case, deciding whether to spend my penny on a piece of Double Bubble gum, a peanut butter log or two caramel squares. Wanda worked the cash register at McCrory's Five and Dime. Wanda had a crush on Eric, so she was nice to me, Eric's little sister, as I examined everything on the shelves. I studied the toys and took dolls down off the shelf, holding them in my arms while imagining taking them home as my own.

It was easier for me to tell Daniel about my past than it was to talk to him about my current challenges. I didn't tell Daniel about my bulimia. I couldn't tell anyone about my vomiting every meal. I was afraid to confess my secret strategy for staying slim. Daniel might insist that I stop vomiting my food. He might report me to the authorities, call in the men in their white suits to carry me away. He seemed the sensible type, like a guy who would be disgusted at the idea of anyone vomiting up every bite of food. I could eat whatever I wanted and not worry about gaining weight, about taking up too much space. I had been vomiting since I was sixteen and I was twenty-six when I entered therapy for the first time. I had no idea what to expect. But people told me therapy was helpful for troubled people. I was troubled.

"Why don't you visit your mother?" Daniel asked at the close of our twelfth weekly session, "See if she can help you remember what happened with the black boy in the field." It was clear Daniel understood very little about my mother and not enough about me. I told him what I thought mattered. It took time, but I learned to tell him things I couldn't tell anyone else.

I told him about my childhood neighbor, Ouida Abbott, who retired from teaching at the University of Florida. The year Edward started kindergarten, I discovered that Dr. Abbott spent a great deal of time in her backyard, which was separated from our backyard by a wire fence, thickly covered with morning glory vines. Since I had no one else to talk to, I talked to Dr. Abbott. And since she had free time, she listened. She was a small woman. She pulled her hair into a loose bun on the back of her head. Wisps of gray hair dangled around her temples. She wore a big straw hat, to shade her face from the Florida sun. I stood on my side of the fence and parted the morning glory vines, so I could see her and watch what she was doing. We talked.

I walked out my kitchen door one day and I could not believe what my eyes saw. Dr. Abbott was standing at the fence with wire pliers in her hand. She was snip-snipping, cutting the wire and vines on that fence. I went running back there, yelling, "Dr. Abbott, this is the kind of thing that can get you in bad trouble!" And she didn't look up. She just kept snip-snipping, cutting that fence, and pulling vines out of her way. Then she pulled the fencing out of the way and gave it a shove. Dr. Abbott stomped down some weeds and stepped right into my backyard. I gasped with delight and hopped over into her backyard.

She invited me to follow her over to a stack of smooth stones, piled against her two-story yellow Victorian house. She picked up a stone and she motioned for me to pick up another stone. I did and I followed her over to that hole she had cut in the fence. She put her stone down and pointed a little further, "Put yours down there." Back and forth we went, picking up stones and laying them down until both of us stood at the foot of the steps that led to Dr. Abbott's kitchen door. "All right," she brushed her hands together, letting the dirt fall to the ground, "this is the way you'll come to visit me every day."

And so, I did. Every day. I went out back and through the opening in the fence and step, step, stepped up to

9

Dr. Abbott's kitchen door. I tilted my head back and hollered through the screen, "Dr. Abbott!"

"Yoo-hoo!" she answered. Sometimes I found her out on the front porch where she would be sitting on a swing, just swinging gently back and forth. I got in the swing beside her. We talked about people walking by on University Boulevard. We talked about people riding by on University Boulevard. Nobody got by without our talking about them. Sometimes I found Dr. Abbott in her library. She had a library all her own with books from the floor to the ceiling on two walls and a red velvet couch on a big round rug in the middle of the room. That couch held us as Dr. Abbott read to me. Some days I found my neighbor way upstairs in her sewing room where she might be whirring away on the sewing machine or sitting in a cozy way, doing needlework. I sat on a hassock and talked while Dr. Abbott sewed. Other days I found her in her kitchen and that made me happiest. She baked her own bread, and she let me help with the baking and the eating of her bread. We played card games at her glass top table or just sat by the kitchen stove and rocked in her green wicker rocking chair. Dr. Abbott really looked at me. She listened to what I had to say. And I loved her. We had a special bond.

I believe that bond and the security I felt in my neighbor's home has much to do with my ability to love myself and enjoy myself now, as an adult, a grandmother and a preacher. Dr. Abbott enjoyed my company from the year I was four until I was twelve years old. She really paid attention to me. She looked at me when I talked, and she laughed when I tried to be funny. She listened carefully. She lit a light deep inside me that has never burned out. I believe I have something to share, something worthwhile to offer the world around me. Currently, I am so well loved. Love and healing cannot be separated in my story. And it was a desire for healing that led me to Daniel's office. I had lost my center.

I told Daniel about Treva Donelson, a cute red head in my first-grade class. She had a sprinkle of fun freckles across her nose. And she liked to play chase on the playground. I was so happy the day Treva walked home from school with me. Her parents had said she could come over and they would pick her up at my house. I wanted Treva to see my dolls and my books and my bed. She liked my things. We put two dolls in a stroller and headed off down the hill to the creek, Sweet Water Branch. The grass was dark green, thick and soft by the creek. Elephant ears drooped from the banks. We left our dolls and our shoes on the grass and slid down into the water. I showed Treva how to catch crawdads in a jar. "Just move the rocks," I nodded, "then get 'em!" She caught one or two and we were laughing about how scary the little crawdads looked, when we both heard something, something that silenced our laughter.

It was a white man with a rain hat on his head. He was calling us. "Hey!" He seemed annoyed.

"Yes sir?"

"See that pencil floating there?" It felt like an accusation.

I looked and saw that there was indeed a pencil in the water. It was turquoise.

"Well, pick it up and give it to me," the man in the rainhat demanded. I did. I grasped the pencil and turned to reach up toward the man, only to see that the man had his penis out of his pants. It was dangling there, dark and ugly, and he was jiggling it as he reached for the pencil. Then he put the pencil in his pants pocket and put his penis away and walked across First Avenue. That's when I turned to see Treva's face. "Let's get out of here!" We climbed out of the creek and ran home, leaving our shoes and my dolls and the strollers.

Treva never came over to my house again. And I wondered if there was something nasty in me, something that attracted nasty men. I wondered if it was safe to trust myself.

I talked with Daniel about my fourth-grade teacher, Mrs. Nelson. She was tall, pencil thin and she had a sharp nose. She wasn't the warm and fuzzy type like Mrs. Holland, my third-grade teacher had been. Mrs. Nelson wouldn't put up with nonsense. She had a ruler on her desk that she used to smack any of us who got out of line. I feared that ruler. I feared Mrs. Nelson. I walked slowly to Kirby Smith Elementary School during that year, dreading the school day and the possibility of becoming the ruler's target.

Mrs. Nelson taught us about diagramming sentences, doing long division and earth sciences. She taught us to look forward to recess, lunch time and the end of the school day. While we played, Mrs. Nelson stood by the fence and smoked cigarettes.

One day, after recess, I was having trouble working on my long division problems. I raised my hand for help and Mrs. Nelson came to my side. She leaned over me and looked at the problem on my worksheet. I smelled the cigarettes on her breath. It seemed like the time was right for me to express my concern. "Mrs. Nelson," I whispered, "ain't you afraid of going to hell?"

"Why, Elaine!" she jerked and stood up straight. "Why would you ask me such a thing?"

"Well, because you smoke cigarettes, and God doesn't allow that kind of nasty habit in heaven."

"I see," she nodded. "Let's worry about your math problems right now. How about that? We can worry about heaven and hell some other time."

Mrs. Nelson told us something I have never forgotten. She told our class that each one of us had the responsibility to keep the earth turning on its axis. "With each step you take, you give the earth the little extra push it needs to stay in motion." I had never heard such a thing, and I felt responsible to get outside and to start walking. I shoved hard against the sidewalk as I walked to and from school.

I told Daniel about the Sunday that my friend, Sally Griner, came home with me after church. Mama had the roast beef in the oven, surrounded by carrots, potatoes and onions. She put rolls on the table along with a plate of pickles and sliced tomatoes. All of us came hungrily to the table. There was a knock on the front door. "Who could that be?" Mama asked as Daddy stood up.

Eric said, "I don't know who it is but hide her," pointing at Sally. "We don't want anybody to think that little pig belongs to us."

Mama and Daddy laughed, "Oh, Eric."

Sally jumped up from the table and ran to my bedroom. I followed her and found her sobbing. "Don't cry. Don't be a baby." I urged her to come back to the table. She refused, insisting on calling her daddy to come get her. From then on, whenever Sally and I played together, I went to her house where I teased her about being a "sissy" and not being rough and tough like me. I had learned to act as if my family's cruelty didn't bother me.

My brother, Edward, was never as rough and tough as the rest of us were at our dinner table. He didn't want us to see his gentle side. More than anything else, Edward wanted to be accepted by the older brothers. The two older boys were Daddy's trophies, his athletes, heartthrobs among the young girls, leaders in the school band. Daddy rarely noticed Edward, skinny, wearing thick glasses from the time he was two and emotionally sensitive. I would've taken up for him, stood by him when the family made fun of him, when the older boys called him "Four Eyes," but I was grasping for any sliver of power I could get in our volatile family dynamic.

I suppose all four of us wanted to be sick, just a little sick, so we could get more motherly warmth. Mama offered sympathy when any of us were sick, and she took on a softer voice. A sort of croon that came with songs while rubbing our head. Special drinks were made and delivered with a flourish. Favorite games were placed beside the bed for when we began to feel better. She read to the one who was sick. She read so well,

15

giving each character their own voice. She was an exuberant reader and so we often fought over who got to be sick.

"You're faking! Mama! He's not sick. He's just wanting to stay home!"

"I am *so* sick! Look. I took my temperature. I'm burning up!"

"He rubbed that thermometer on the wool blanket, Mama!"

Even if we wanted to be at school, for some peculiar reason, we did not want any of our siblings to get the chance to stay home. It was always a zero-sum game. Her charm and her eyes were focused on Daddy. She went along with him wherever he went and watched him so closely that he never had to say he needed something. Mama, a devoted wife, thought ahead for Daddy. And she crouched behind their chest of drawers, with her eyes covered, when he took off his belt and beat me in their bedroom.

I hid my face with my hands as I told Daniel about the beatings. I can still feel the shame. Daddy undressed me before he beat me, and I was left with whelps all over my legs, buttocks and back. I wore long pants and long sleeves when I went to school, covering up my shame.

I told Daniel about camp meeting, the church camp our family attended for a week every summer while we were in Florida. Church camp was a time for Nazarenes from all over the state of Florida to get together just outside White Springs. Camp meeting was all about praising the Lord. My older brothers spent their week looking for girls with big breasts and nice legs. I knew what they wanted because I heard them talking about girls. Once they had a girlfriend, they sat with her at worship services, bought her ice cream treats at the snack stand and walked together down the dirt road to the old cemetery. Daytime hours at camp were filled with softball games, horseshoes being slung, meals in the noisy dining hall, and Bible study.

The main event of every day at camp meeting was the evening worship service. Song evangelists whipped the crowd up into a heated frenzy. Worship services at camp included shouting, waving of arms and dashing round and round the tabernacle. Men took off their t-shirts and waved them over their heads as they ran for the glory of the Lord. My mother and father didn't run or shout much. They were more reserved Nazarenes. But my mother was one of the women who went down to the altar to pray with people when the preacher gave the call for sinners to come forward and be cleansed. Mama knelt with people, put her hands on their backs and asked the Lord to hear their prayers.

Mr. and Mrs. Spence, a rich couple who came to camp meeting every summer in a fancy Cadillac, owned motels down in Orlando. Mr. Spence was an unusual Nazarene because he had money. Most of our Nazarene friends were just getting by on what the Lord allowed. Mr. and Mrs. Spence stayed in the nicest cabin on the camp-grounds, and everybody treated them as if they were royalty.

The summer I was four, Mrs. Spence asked my mother for permission to take me into White Springs to shop at J C Penney's. "We'd like to buy Elaine something nice to wear, a Sunday dress," she said. My mother was busy working as the camp's registrar, and she was happy to have someone else look after me for a while. As a preacher's family, we were accustomed to people giving us hand-me-downs to wear. Having something new and store-bought would be a treat.

"Let's hope she doesn't talk both your legs off on the ride into town and back." Mama waved her hand and turned back to the work on her desk. Mr. Spence lifted me up off the floor and carried me to his car.

Mr. and Mrs. Spence sat in the front seat, and I slid around on the leather backseat. It was the air-conditioner that fascinated me most. No hot air blowing through open windows; the Cadillac windows were closed. Cold air was blowing against the back of my head.

Mrs. Spence asked me what size dress I wore. "My mama knows," I responded.

"Well, your mama is not here now so we'll have to find out what dress size fits a chubby girl like you." I winced at the sound. I knew I was too fat; my brothers called me Fatso. "There's no need for us to get a dress that doesn't fit, right?" Mrs. Spence turned around and I admired the way her long hair was braided and then twisted beautifully round her head. My long blonde hair was forever tangled and unruly, even when it was braided. Mama had pulled my hair into a ponytail just before the Spence's picked me up.

Mr. Spence turned quickly, giving me a stern glance, "If you're a good girl today we'll get a pretty dress for you to wear to church next Sunday." He pulled off the highway and rolled to a stop in front of a motel. "I'll be right back."

It didn't look to me like a place where dresses were sold. Mrs. Spence looked over her shoulder and said, "Now you be a good girl." Her eyes fell to my skinned knees and the dirt on my feet. "We'll need to get you cleaned up before you can try on dresses."

Mr. Spence returned to the car and opened the back door. "Come on."

He unlocked the door, and I followed him into a room with two beds and a desk. Mrs. Spence took my hand and pulled me to the bathroom. "Let's get your clothes off and get you in this tub," she pulled my t-shirt up and I raised my arms. Then the Spences did things with me and my body that no child should ever see or experience.

Mr Spence's breath smelled like dog doodoo. He slapped the back of my head. I knew that a slap to the head was just the beginning. Angry men give girls a slap before they make fists or pull their belt out of its loops. I was scared to death of Daddy's anger and his belt. I was scared to death of Mr. Spence.

After a few moments Mr. Spence collapsed on top of me, knocking the wind out of me. Mrs. Spence saw that I had lost my breath. "Get off her!" He raised himself on his elbows and I gasped, choking before I got back to breathing.

He sat up and looked at me, huffing through his mouth, raising one eyebrow. "Now you were not as good a girl as I had hoped you'd be but Mrs. Spence and I will get you a new dress. Right, honey?"

She was pulling up her hose and connecting them to garter snaps. "Right sweetie."

"Even though you were a disappointment, we'll go on into town. You can pick something out at J C Penney's.

20

But you are never," he put his face up against my face, "to talk about this room and how we had fun together. Because if you do, I'll have to tell your mama and daddy that their chubby little girl isn't good enough for any more shopping trips. I might have to tell them how bad you've been and how stinky you are."

Shame and confusion washed over me like hot lead. It cooled, hardened and stuck to me. When we returned to the campground, Edward was sitting under an oak tree, watching men play horseshoes. He got up and came toward me as I carried my sack with a new dress, a new crinoline, socks, and black patent leather shoes. "What'd you do, to get all that?" He frowned. I knew he was mad because nobody had invited him to go shopping at J C Penney's. I didn't tell him or anyone about what I had done to get those new clothes. I told no one about Mr. and Mrs. Spence.

# MOVING AFTER DADDY DIED

D aniel sat and waited, his hands clasped in his lap, while we shared silence. He had listened and because he was not disgusted by me, I started to cry. His office was a safe place to have feelings. I was trying to make sense of my life. Daniel's small office held big feelings for me.

*The experience with the Spence's taught me that my body was not my own. It didn't belong to me. Decisions were not mine to make regarding who could touch me and where they could touch me. The boundaries were blurred into nothingness. Only love has healed those wounds, the love of neighbors, teachers, friends and partners. I have been fortunate, and I know it. I live with all the privileges that come with living as an able-bodied white woman in an urban area where being homosexual is largely accepted. Learning to respect my body has been an ongoing struggle.*

Right after I started sixth grade, Daddy accepted a call from God to move all of us to Lakeland, Florida where he would be the pastor for South Florida Heights Church of the Nazarene. We moved seventy miles away from Gainesville and I lost contact with Dr. Abbott and my friends at church and at Kirby Smith Elementary School.

Daniel knew about my daddy's death. That was a part of my story I shared on the first few therapy sessions, how death had come to our new house in Lakeland, two days after Christmas. I was eleven when a heart attack snatched daddy. He was forty-six. That left everybody's heads swirling with nowhere to go, no way to imagine life without a preacher in the house. It was 1963, and we lived in the parsonage, a home owned by the church and loaned to the preacher's family for as long as the man of the house was their preacher. Mama had no job other than playing the piano in church every Sunday and Wednesday night. She made the church newsletter and mailed it out. I figured we would soon starve, and nobody told me any different. When word got out that Daddy was dead, Mrs. Fulwood stood at our kitchen sink, managing all the casseroles, salads and cakes that poured through the front door. I heard her say to Mrs. Grainger, "Well this was just God's will, and we can't question that." I wondered how it could be God's will, having us kicked out of our house and left with no money for food. We were good people. How could God treat us so badly? But Mama, without my knowing, had a plan and strong faith. I soon learned just how strong and determined she could be.

As the widow of a Nazarene minister, my mother was known in Nazarene circles. She got several offers to join the faculty at Nazarene colleges. She had her master's degree in English from the University of Florida, so it turned out she could teach. We wouldn't starve after all. Edward and I were the only kids still living at home. Eric was married and attending college and Eugene was working a job in Chicago. Mama left Edward and me with our grandparents, while she flew to Nashville, Tennessee and accepted a teaching position at Trevecca Nazarene College. While she was there, she signed papers to buy a home for us on Elysian Fields Road, a nice brick house on a corner lot with a driveway that circled around back. She got the job and a house, then she came back to Lakeland and contacted a driver's education school because she needed to learn how to drive. Daddy's Buick Le Sabre was collecting dust, sitting next to Grandpa's citrus grove.

We lived in a little rented house next door to Grandma and Grandpa the year between Daddy's death and our move to Nashville. Grandpa forbade us to walk through his lawn. He was certain our socks and shoes carried sandspur seeds. "Walk on the sidewalk!" he hollered at us if we dared to cross over his yard. "I'll tan your hide if I catch you on this grass!" He spent a good portion of every day on his knees, pulling weeds. I thought it was part of his religion. Grandpa in his work pants on his knees with Jesus, saving his beloved Bermuda grass from the evils of dandelions and sand spurs.

I told Daniel about our family's move from Florida to Tennessee. Mama got behind the wheel of Daddy's Buick and began our drive from Lakeland, Florida to Nashville. I sat in the front seat beside her holding my Chatty Kathy doll, wondering what life would be like in our new home, where I would go to school and who would be my new friends. Edward and Eugene were ahead of us in a U-Haul truck. Eugene was driving and he left us far behind. A new and cautious driver, Mama and I only made it as far as Valdosta, Georgia that first day. We spent the night in a motel and got up early to continue our journey north.

The second afternoon of our trip turned stormy. I watched as pine trees bent and whipped back and forth in the wind. Rain fell hard at a slant as our windshield wipers slapped back and forth. Mama kept her eyes strained straight ahead on the two-lane highway as we entered Monteagle, Tennessee. I could feel her nervous energy and I wished I could do something to help besides just sitting quietly beside her. Then she pulled over to the side of the road and stopped the car. "Elaine, I'm lost. I think we should have taken another road back there but I'm not sure." She reached for my hand. "Will you say a prayer for us?" She bowed her head and closed her eyes.

"Dear God," my voice cracked. Rain pelted the car as the wind rocked it. "Help us find our way to our new home. Keep us safe. Help Mama not to be afraid. Amen."

And then my mother started quoting the 91st Psalm. She knew so much scripture by heart.

*You who live in the shelter of the Most High, who abide in the shadow of the Almighty, will say to the Lord, "My refuge and my fortress; my God in whom I trust." For he will deliver you from the snare of the fowler and from the deadly pestilence; he will cover you with his pinions, and under his wings you will find refuge; his faithfulness is a shield and buckler. You will not fear the terror of the night, or the arrow that flies by day, or the pestilence that stalks in darkness, or the destruction that wastes at noonday.*

She took a deep breath and squeezed my hand. And she started the car again. After driving several miles, Mama stopped again at a restaurant. We ran inside and shook the rain off as we were ushered to a table. We both got a grilled cheese sandwich and a cup of soup. Mama ordered two scoops of chocolate ice cream for me. While I ate my sweet treat, she talked with the waitress about directions and which highway to take.

The rain had stopped when we went outside again. Mama held written instructions for how to get where we were going. At ten o'clock that night we passed a sign that said, "Nashville City Limits." We were on the Nolensville Road and Mama recognized where we were. She turned onto the Elysian Fields Road and found the house she had bought for us. Eugene and Edward had emptied the truck of all our furniture and belongings. "Where were you? What took you so long?" Eugene asked. Mama fussed at Eugene for leaving

26

us behind, but mostly we were all glad to be safe and together in our new home.

I currently live with a profound faith that all will be well. I have grown to a place where I see the world as benevolent. That kind of faith has taken time, much time spent in prayer and many hours in therapy. I am loving and compassionate and I expect the same from the outside world. I don't know much but I know that love created everything that exists, and love will redeem it all in the end. I trust that good things are ahead because I am surrounded by goodness now.

I realized I was wasting Daniel's time and my own time by not talking about my eating disorder. So, I put the black boy on a back burner once again, took a deep breath and revealed how I related to food. To talk about the black boy and what I remembered about him would mean I had to accuse my own family of doing horrible things. I preferred to talk about the horrible things I had done myself. There was plenty for me to confess.

It began in high school, during the summer after my sophomore year. Mama had remarried. Our stepfather, Jim, was a Nazarene preacher like Daddy. He moved us from

Nashville to Hendersonville where he served a church. Mama drove into town to teach her classes at the college.

Sandy Adams was my best friend. She was prettier than I was. I was glad to be best friends with a girl who was perfect looking. It was a way for me to be valuable too. She taught me how to apply make-up and I recognized how ineffective the powder and paint were on my face. I was nowhere near being considered pretty. I was, however, a good and loyal friend. Sandy and I swam together in Saunders Ferry Lake. We baby sat together and worked side by side as waitresses at her family's restaurant, Saunders Ferry Boat Dock and Café.

We served fried catfish and French fries to people who owned boats at the dock. It was a popular place on the weekends. Sandy's mother delivered the beer to our customers since we were too young to serve beer. Sandy and I competed on Friday and Saturday nights, seeing who could earn the most tips. She usually won because the guys were attracted to her and tipped her well for an extra smile or two. The work gave us spending money which we used to buy make-up, jewelry and clothes in the downtown shops in Hendersonville.

One man, Richard Mallory, always tipped us generously. Sandy and I scurried to get his order when he wandered over to a table. He was always alone. No wife. No friends. But a good-looking man with a head full of black hair and brown eyes. He seemed dark and mysterious. One Friday evening after I served Richard his dinner and after I put his five-dollar tip in my pocket, he put his hand on my hip and smiled broadly. "How about coming with me for a boat ride? We can have some fun."

"And Sandy too?" I looked at her across the dining room, knowing she would not want to be left out.

"She can find her own fun," he winked. "You and I will be enough."

And so it was that I got into Richard's boat. The sun had set, and Saunders Ferry Lake was smooth. He started the boat, and the smell of motor oil filled my nose as we pulled away from the dock. Richard drove us out into the middle of the lake and then he idled the engine. He moved to sit beside me at the back of the boat. From a cooler, he lifted a can of Miller High Life beer and offered it to me as if drinking beer was a normal thing to do. I had never tasted it, but I did my best to act grown up as I swallowed. Then he kissed me. "Let's enjoy being alone out here," he urged me. He popped the top of his own beer and took a long drink, looking at me in the moonlight. Richard was attracted to me, not Sandy. I felt like I was stealing something that rightly belonged to a prettier girl.

We drank our beer and watched the moon rise as gentle waves slapped against the side of the boat. Richard put his arm around me and pulled me closer. He kissed me again and touched my breast.

The night air was warm and heavy as Richard showed me how to touch him and give him pleasure. Then he sat up and zipped his jeans. I reached for my jeans, suddenly feeling a chill. As I pulled them on, I dared to ask, "Are you my boyfriend now?"

"Oh," he stood up and walked to the steering wheel. "No honey. You're not my type at all. My girlfriends are much older than you." I was fourteen. He opened the boat's engine, and we roared back toward the dock. He didn't say it, but I knew his girlfriends were much prettier and slimmer than me. I couldn't change my face, but I could lose weight and be slimmer.

# EATING DISORDER

I went on a diet to lose fifteen pounds with a goal weight of 115 pounds. I hoped I had a chance, at that weight, to become Richard's real girlfriend. I hoped, if I lost weight, I might be somebody's girlfriend, anybody's girlfriend. I saw myself as fat for my five feet and four inches of height. I cut out sweets, stopped eating a honey bun every afternoon after school and cut back on my portions at each meal. My mother encouraged my diet, offering to do calisthenics with me every evening just before we had dinner. "Jumping jacks, ready?" We rattled the plates and cups in the china cabinet with our jumping and running in place. I lost fifteen pounds within a few months of trying and Mama was so proud of me. I started eating less. I kept a file card for each day, writing down what I ate and how many calories I had taken in. I ate a grapefruit for breakfast, an orange and fish sticks for lunch and a lettuce wedge with French dressing and a skinned chicken breast for dinner. That was my habit until I learned to cut out the fish sticks and chicken breasts. Weight began to pour off me as I increased my daily exercise to include a four-mile run through the park behind our house.

I enjoyed baking sweets for my family, and I got satisfaction by watching them eat cookies, pies, and cakes that

I made. Edward especially appreciated my divinity, so I made that for him every weekend.

From the very beginning of Mama's marriage to Jim, he made it clear that he distrusted Edward and me. "Your children," he pointed his finger at us while he talked to my mother, "are your biggest problem." And Mama didn't argue the point. Her grim silence on the matter worried me. I heard their bed banging against the wall at night and I knew that Jim had something to offer Mama, something she wanted more than she wanted us to be comfortable in our own home. My brother grew so frustrated with Jim, his constant accusations and his threats to punish us that Edward punched holes in the wall of his bedroom. I focused on eating less. Mama focused on grading papers. Jim sat in his Lazy Boy recliner and watched television.

I took piano lessons from Ruby Felker, a member of our church. She provided a lesson for me every Monday afternoon in exchange for my watching her little girls while she gave lessons to three other students. It worked for both of us. I just wanted to know how to play hymns so I could play piano for our church services.

Mama and I were running in place when the kitchen phone rang. "Oh, hello Ruby," I heard my mother say. Then there was silence for several minutes. "I hear you. Yes. I will do something about it. Goodbye."

"What was that about?" Jim asked from his recliner in the den.

"That was Ruby Felker, and she accused me of being a negligent parent." My mother wasn't looking at me, but she was glaring at her husband who sat watching the television. "Do you hear me? She says if I don't take Elaine to see a doctor, she's going to report me to children's services for abuse. Get in here right now, young lady!" At that time, I weighed eighty-five pounds, and my goal was to weigh eighty-three pounds. I could still pinch fat around my waist; my thighs spread out when I sat on the toilet. I wanted that extra flesh to go away.

My mother and her husband focused on me. "We're not going to stand for this kind of thing. You understand?" Mama motioned for me to follow her into the hallway where she stood in front of the full-length mirror. "Now I want you to look at yourself. Just look at yourself. I want you to start eating and stop this stubborn dieting. You understand?"

"I'm sorry Mama. But I'm still fat."

"Fat! What fat?"

"Right here and here."

"Oh, for Pete's sake! You look like those starving children in Bangladesh. I'm taking you to see a doctor and you're going to do your part by eating more."

"I can't eat."

"You most certainly will eat, and I'll see to that."

"Ok. Ok." I sighed with relief. I was glad the awful confrontation was over, and I was glad to be going to a doctor. I wasn't lying to my mother; I couldn't eat. There had been times lately when I was so scared by the smell of death's breath against my neck that I had sat down at the dinner table, planning to eat. But then my hands would begin to shake, and my guts quaked. Cold sweat beaded all over my body. Nothing in me had the courage to challenge that refusal to eat. I looked forward to seeing a doctor; the sooner the better.

I only had to wait a couple days before Dr. Winston worked me into his schedule. A general practitioner, I had never seen him before. His nurse asked me to undress and put on a paper gown. Then she assisted me to the end of the exam table. It was cold in the room and my skin looked blue. Dark circles surrounded my eyes. My inner ankle bones were bruised and bloody where the two bones had knocked into each other over the last few months. My hair was fragile and falling out by handfuls from lack of protein. The doctor walked in.

He was old, gray with tufts of hair coming out his nose and ears. "Hello, Mrs. Eades," he turned to greet my mother. "What have we got here?" He went from shaking my mother's hand to looking at a written record on a clipboard. "Not eating. Hmmmmm."

He sat down on his rolling stool and slid over to me. Looking right into my eyes, he put his hands on my bony knees. "Honey, have you got problems with your mother?"

"Well, I never! Problems with her mother! What kind of doctor are you anyway? If we needed a psychiatrist, I would have taken her to see one. We're going! Get dressed, Elaine."

I never got the chance to tell Dr. Winston how hard it was for me to earn my mother's approval. I didn't have a chance to tell him how my daddy had died and how my mother had abandoned me for love of her new husband.

We got in the car. Fuming, Mama said, "Well, that visit certainly will not satisfy Ruby. I'll find another doctor. We'll go into Nashville for a real professional."

Dr. Phillips, an internist, was part of Vanderbilt Medical School's teaching practice. A few days later, I sat in his office.

It was a nice room, shadowed with thick draperies and carpeted. My chair was leather and so was the chair my mother sat in. She explained to Dr. Phillips, "Elaine has lost weight and says she can't eat. So, I need for you to tell her that she can eat. There's no medical condition preventing her eating, is there? If you ask me, she's just plain stubborn; always has been."

Dr. Phillips looked at me. His gaze was kind and open. "Do you think you have a medical condition, Elaine?" It was the spring of 1968, years before terms like anorexia nervosa, bulimia and eating disorder were in common use.

"I don't know. Maybe. I just can't eat."

Dr. Phillips accepted that and pushed a button on his intercom, inviting his nurse to come in. "Take Elaine with you, please. Let's get a CBC and an SMA-18. Then bring her back here. Thanks." I was comforted by the warmth in Dr. Phillip's voice. When the results of my blood tests came back, Dr. Phillips said I needed to be admitted to the hospital immediately. My potassium level was extremely low.

Not eating had evolved into my identity, my personal power. Being thin was a strategy I hoped would earn my mother's approval. She valued self-discipline over every other virtue. My practice of not eating inspired my mother's admiration as well as her anger. I could see both in her eyes as an orderly came to take me across the breezeway to the hospital.

Following the paper-signing at admissions, I was rolled in a wheelchair to the elevator. My mother was running to keep up. When the elevator doors closed, my mother began to wring her hands. The elevator was crowded, and the group's silence must have felt like an indictment on her parenting. "I just don't know what to think about how crowded this hospital is. My daughter is being put on the psychiatric floor because there aren't any beds available on the other floors." I looked at my shoes with an intense heat pouring over my embarrassed body.

We got to my assigned room, and I saw a woman sitting in the window, staring out. "Margaret, this is Elaine, your roommate," the nurse gave introductions even though Margaret never turned her head to look our way. Margaret wore a brightly colored moo-moo. Her hair, long and coal black with an inch of gray roots showing, was flying about from the air-conditioner breeze below the sill where she was sitting.

"Well," Mama addressed the nurse, "looks like you know what to do here. I need to get to my class; I teach at Trevecca Nazarene College. You know the school?" The nurse was helping me get out of my street clothes and into a hospital gown. She allowed as how she didn't recognize the name of the school. She wore a crisp white uniform, and a white nursing cap. Mama walked to the door. "I'll come back tomorrow, honey. Now you do what they say, you understand?" She raised an eyebrow at me as if I might argue, and then she was gone.

The nurse covered me with a sheet and fluffed the pillow behind my head. "Dr. Phillips will be by to see you later this evening. He has ordered several meds and some tests. So, you just relax and I'm going to start an IV, give you some fluids intravenously. That's the most important thing right now. The fluid will have potassium in it and that's what your body needs." She was cheerful and reassuring. I settled down under the sheet.

There were many tubes of blood sucked out of my veins followed by a ride to ultrasound for an abdominal scan. Then I relaxed, as the nurse had directed me to do, watching afternoon television. That evening Dr. Phillips came by with an entourage of medical students. They formed a half circle around my bed as Dr. Phillips placed his stethoscope on my throat, my chest, my abdomen. He had me grip his fingers and push against his shove. He investigated my ears and eyes. I was falling in love with him, his brown eyes and his white coat as he examined me. His kindness satisfied something hungry in me. One of the medical students asked me to get out of bed, stand beside it and perform a deep knee bend.

"Hmmmm," it was uttered in unison as I did the exercise without effort.

I had an enema that night to get ready for a barium swallow and barium enema scheduled for the next day. I felt embarrassed with so much attention being paid to my rear end. But I was soaking up the kindness of the medical staff. Margaret ignored me completely.

The first morning of my hospital stay, I woke up with a weary smile. The nursing assistant patted my shoulder. "Wake up, honey. We need to get your vital signs, and we need you to come out to the nurses' station so we can get you on the scales and see how much you weigh."

"Do you have to weigh me?" I looked for an escape. "I weighed before I left home. I can tell you what I weigh. 83 pounds." I couldn't hide my pride. It had been a long, determined journey. Days of writing down less and less on the index cards I kept for each day's diet and weight. Eating less than five hundred calories a day was a good day. Weighing anything below ninety pounds would obviously be considered thin. I was confident nobody could argue about that. My weight was the measure of my worth.

"Oh, sweety, we will be weighing you every morning. Let's get you up without dislodging your IV line, shall we?

Let me help you." She attached the liter of fluid to a rolling pole and then she carefully assisted me out of bed and supported me as I walked. It was funny to me, to be treated as though I was sick. I giggled nervously and looked around for witnesses to this charade. I stepped on the scale. The nursing assistant read my weight out loud, "86 pounds." And she started to write that down in my chart. But I slapped the chart out of her hands and leaped off the scale toward her. As the chart skittered down the linoleum floor, I yanked the IV line out of my forearm and shouted, "No way! No way! No way you people are gonna make me gain weight. No way! No way!" Blood was running from the back of my hand. Every time I said *No way* I jumped and stomped my feet as vigorously as possible.

"Sweety! Calm down. Calm down, honey." She was trying to get hold of my hand with a roll of gauze.

"I am not a sweety or a honey! I am somebody who is not going to get fat. You understand?"

When breakfast trays came, I had only clear liquids. I brushed the entire tray off my over-bed table and enjoyed the splash and clatter. It woke Margaret who got out of bed and came over to me. She grabbed both of my cheeks and squeezed them while staring into my eyes with a wide toothy grin. "Let's dance, girly!"

She led me around the spilled tray and its contents over to her side of the room. Then she grabbed my right hand and, putting her other hand on my hip, she began to trot around the room, pulling me along, swaying as we went. Margaret was singing, "Dancing with a dolly with a hole in her stocking and her knees kept a knockin,' and her toes kept a rockin'! Dancing with a dolly with a hole in her stockin' and we danced by the light of the moon. Yes, we danced by the light of the moon." The nurse, an orderly and several medical students were standing in the doorway as we trotted to a stop. The nursing assistant came in the room, not looking at either Margaret or me. She just started cleaning up the breakfast mess. I didn't offer to help her. And no one tried to restart any intravenous fluid on me.

I had an upper GI, which is an examination of the pharynx, esophagus, stomach and first part of my small intestine. A gastroenterologist did that test, and he did a colonoscopy on me the following day after a rigorous cleaning out regimen. A gynecologist did a pelvic exam, and I hated that so much hot tears poured out of my eyes and slid across my temples and into my hair. I managed not to sob out loud. Not everything at the hospital was like a vacation. Some of it was worse than my stepfather's silent treatment and scornful looks. Some of it made me want to go home and hide.

Just after they delivered my evening tray, the television announced breaking news. Dr. Martin Luther King Jr. had been assassinated in Memphis. Margaret sat up in her bed. She looked over at me. Then she came over and crawled into my bed, putting one arm around my shoulders. We watched the breaking news together.

Dr. Phillips came by the last night of my hospital stay. He sat on my bed and looked at me for a while, not saying a word. Then, "They tell me you are eating only lettuce and fresh fruit. That all you want?"

I nodded.

"Could I talk you into eating some chicken or beef?"

"I allow myself to eat roasted chicken sometimes, couple times a month."

"If I order some roasted chicken right now, get it sent up from the cafeteria, will you eat it?"

"I would."

"Well then, since I'm ordering and getting a delivery made to this room, how about we ask for some dessert?"

I frowned. "No sugar. Can't do it."

"What is your favorite dessert, if you allowed yourself to eat sugar?"

"Blackberry cobbler."

"Oh, I do love blackberry cobbler! How about I order some and if you don't want it, I'll eat it? That allowable?"

Dr. Phillips went to see other patients while we waited for our nighttime snack to arrive. The nurses called him when they saw the tray delivered. He returned and pulled a chair up to sit beside me. "I hope you don't mind if I just sit here and enjoy the sight of you eating that chicken. I've been so looking forward to this treat."

I laughed at his silliness and took a bite of the thigh after stripping away the skin.

"I thought you might want to read these articles I found in some of my research." Dr. Phillips handed over some sheets of paper. "These are articles about a condition some doctors have seen, a condition called anorexia nervosa. I don't know, but I thought you might read the articles and consider if what those doctors have seen is anything like what I am seeing in you."

"Anorexia nervosa?" I had read about it in a women's magazine.

"Yes. The one article tells of religious women devoted to starving themselves as a way to express their dedication to God, starving themselves in an effort to get closer to God."

He could see I was considering that. "You take those home with you tomorrow, read them and see if you learn anything helpful from what those doctors have seen." I couldn't make myself eat the blackberry cobbler, so Dr. Phillips ate it and told me stories about his family. He clearly loved his wife and three sons, and he clearly enjoyed the cobbler.

My mother came to pick me up at 11:00 the following day and the discharge process was inexplicably delayed for such a long time that Mama was missing her World Literature class. "Those freshmen will be delighted to miss class," she fretted and paced. Margaret had been discharged the day before, so it was just the two of us waiting. "Well, all I can say is I hope Ruby Felker is happy now. I mean, what else am I supposed to do? As far as I can see, nothing has changed. The nurses tell me you're still not eating. They gave you some fluids and ran some tests and now they'll charge us an arm and a leg to pay for all of this nonsense." She walked to the door as though looking for answers. She turned, "Can you explain to me why on earth you are being so stubborn?"

"I am not being stubborn," I sobbed.

"Well, I don't know what you call it then. Maybe head strong? Because you are certainly fine mentally. This is not some kind of disease unless you consider being head strong a disease. I'm not going to put up with this; you hear me? Jim and I are going to General Assembly in Kansas City; we're leaving in the morning. We'll stay with your Aunt Eunice and Uncle Larry. And we'll be back in a week. I want you to use that time to consider what you're doing by refusing to eat. Just think about it. And I expect you to be ready to eat by the time we get home. Jim has lost all patience with you, and he's tired of seeing what you're doing to me with this behavior."

The next morning, Edward and I waved as Mama and Jim backed out the driveway in his fast-back Barracuda. Edward was perched on the patio steps out back, cleaning his rifle. I went inside and put a record on my player, "Sitting on the Dock of the Bay" by Otis Redding. The music soothed me and brought tears to my eyes. I bent over my dresser to take a close, very close, look at myself. My eyes looked sunken, set deep behind bony dark circles. My long blonde hair was brittle and frizzy. And the tendons along my neck were exposed like tight ropes, bulging through fragile, easily bruised, skin.

"You're going to die," I wasn't sure if I said it out loud or if I was hearing voices. I knew it was true, no matter who was talking. Leaning in toward the mirror, I looked straight into my reflection. I could see that I didn't really want to die; I just didn't want to live my life anymore.

"Edward," I took the needle off the record and burst out of my bedroom. "Edward! Do you want some pancakes?" I knew he did; Edward never turned down pancakes. I was planning to eat with him. Mama was right; I had been head-strong. Surely, I could eat a little something.

I made pancakes and put a stack on his plate. Then I turned to make more. "Hey! Really. Don't make any more. This is all I want." Edward gestured at his plate where butter was melting and running down the sides of the pancake, syrup flowed lazily, dripping down the stack.

"No. I'm making some for me." I didn't have to turn and look at Edward to know he was surprised.

"Oh, ok then."

I put butter and syrup on my pancakes, a stack of two as large as the dinner plate they sat on. I poured myself a tall glass of milk and tipped it up before I could change my mind. I could feel Edward eyeing me as I ate a first bite and then a second. The butter and syrup oozed down my throat with the warm pancake. I cleaned the plate and then I looked up. It was then that the panic took over. My teeth started chattering as if I were naked in a snowstorm, the palms of my hands got slick with sweat and I suddenly felt like I couldn't breathe, couldn't breathe, can't… "I'm gonna be sick," I raced from the kitchen to the bathroom, slammed the door shut and hurled the entire contents of my stomach into the toilet. As instantly as I had fallen into a panic, so instantly did my panic disappear. "I'm fine," I hollered at Edward who was outside the door acting like some old, worried lady.

"Elaine, are you ok in there? Don't you up and die on me while Mama and Jim aren't here."

The trembling and sweating stopped. I took a deep breath and flushed the toilet.

It became my secret; I could eat and vomit. That became my way to avoid panic. I could please others by eating. And I could please myself by flushing the food down the toilet.

Daniel didn't call in the authorities and he didn't look disgusted about my vomiting. He asked, "And what does it feel like now, having told me about your vomiting?"

"I feel afraid you're going to try to force me to stop vomiting."

"You're afraid I will become your mother?"

I hadn't noticed, but I did expect the whole world to react toward me like my mother.

"I'm not your mother and I will not force you to do anything you are not ready to do. But I do wonder if you might consider in-patient treatment, just a break from the marriage and mothering." Both of his eyebrows were raised and that scared me. "Why not let some others take care of you while you maybe look at loving your body rather than punishing it?" He was leaning toward me.

"No. But thank you for your concern." I called and canceled my next appointment with Daniel. My paranoia kicked in. I had come too close to being sent to the psych ward again, where they might weigh me every day, watch what I eat, and go to the bathroom with me to make sure I didn't vomit. I let Daniel go.

The singer, Karen Carpenter, died in 1983, suffering from complications brought on by her eating disorder. Suddenly anorexia and bulimia were in the news. I worried that people might guess how I stayed so thin. My family and friends watched me eating large portions of food. They commented on the mystery of how I managed my weight. I resented Karen Carpenter, and I hoped Daniel wouldn't come knocking on our door. The men in their white coats had never felt so close to becoming a reality.

# THE BOOK OF ROMANS
## AND MESCALINE

I n October of 1969, my stepfather accepted a call to move us from Hendersonville to Jackson, Tennessee where he served as pastor for First Nazarene Church and where Edward and I started attending high school. We were both seniors. I made no effort to make new friends. I spent my lunch hour in the classroom with Mrs. Johnson, my English teacher. Mrs. Johnson was new to the school too. She was the first black teacher assigned to teach at the all-white school. Neither one of us had any friends at the school. We spent the hour together. I always brought fruit to eat, and she brought a sandwich. Sometimes we talked and sometimes we sat in silence and read, appreciating a safe place to be.

Twice each month the clubs were scheduled to meet during homeroom, after the lunch hour. I had no interest in joining a club, so I sat at my desk and read while others scurried off to enjoy extracurricular activities. Carolyn Brown was in my homeroom. She worked on the school's newspaper and was on the yearbook council. She took an interest in my lack of interest and began pestering me on club days. "Come on. You can't hide behind a book for the rest of your life. Let go and have a little fun! Come to my club with me." One club day she embarrassed me more than usual; her pestering was drawing unwanted attention from other kids. I stood up and shouted, "Ok!" Then I followed her downstairs to the auditorium where she introduced me to the others in her club, Thespians.

The group was friendly, accepting me as one of them and inviting me to help plan and perform the senior play. On the following club day, I didn't have to be coerced into heading for the auditorium. The theater group quickly became my group. I was cast in a leading role for the senior play, and I got busy learning my lines. When I asked my mother to help by running lines with me, she knitted her brows and reminded me, "Honey, we don't support the theater. Our church teaches that's where Satan hangs out and causes all kinds of problems for people." I learned my lines in my own room with the door closed. None of my family came to see the senior play and I was sorry about that. I was just relieved that my mother didn't forbid me to be in the play. Something inside me was awakened by the chance to perform, to be somebody other than myself for an hour or two. I was having fun.

Carolyn told me that the Jackson Theatre Guild was holding auditions for a play called "Oliver." She didn't have time to be in another play, but I did. Carolyn drove me to the junior high school where the auditions were taking place. Waving to Carolyn, I ran inside where a long line of little boys stood, each of them holding sheets of music. As each boy took the stage, he handed the pianist his music and began to sing. Standing in line, I asked the little boy next to me, "Does everybody have to sing a song for this play?" The answer was yes, and I started wracking my brain for something to sing besides a hymn. The songs I knew best didn't seem like the right choice. When it was my turn, I asked the pianist, "Do you know how to play *You're a Grand Ol' Flag*? He did know how to play it and I belted it out for all I was worth. Jesse Byrum, the director, howled with laughter and applauded wildly. The director gave me the part of Bette, and I had so much fun with that group of community theater people. They embraced me, gave me rides to rehearsals and when I graduated from high school the theatre guild awarded me a scholarship to study theater at a small local college. I made up my mind to study theater where I figured I could take my chances with Satan. I had found myself in the theater and I liked what I had found.

It was 1970, and I was a skinny freshman who had had no experience of the world outside of my very Nazarene home. I carried my Bible to my dorm room along with my strict notions of what it meant to be a Christian. As a reaction to my shame about vomiting every meal, I focused on being good. I taught Sunday school and studied my Bible. I spent time in daily prayer and wrote religious poetry. My roommate, Lynsey, was a basketball player from up north. We stuck close together during those first few weeks at college. During Rush Week, Lynsey and I were both invited to join a sorority, Alpha Xi Delta. We joined and they instantly made me chaplain of the pledge class. I was that kind of kid.

I ate lunch one day and returned to my dorm room, wondering why I hadn't seen Lynsey in the cafeteria. I opened the door to our room and my eyes could not believe what they saw there. Lynsey was on her knees at the end of her bed and her sorority big sister, Brenda, was sitting on the end of the bed and they were locked in a hot romantic embrace. A long stem rose was on the floor beside them. I backed out of the room and leaned against the wall. "Oh no. Oh no." I could hardly breathe.

Lynsey raced into the hallway, "Elaine…come in here. It's ok. It's ok."

But it was not ok in my mind. As soon as my shock wore off and turned into rage, I went door to door in that freshman dorm, asking all the Alpha Xi Delta pledges to come to the sorority room that night. Then I stood on a stool before all the gathered pledges and investigated their faces. I reported to them what I had seen in my own room earlier that day and I read to them from the book of Romans:

*Romans, Chapter 1 Verses 24-27*

*Therefore, God gave them up in the lusts of their heart to impurity, to the degrading of their bodies among themselves, because they exchanged the truth about God for a lie and worshiped and served the creature rather than the Creator, who is blessed forever. Amen. For this reason, God gave them up to degrading passions. Their women exchanged natural intercourse for unnatural, and in the same way also the men, giving up natural intercourse with women, were consumed with passion for one another. Men committed shameless acts with men and received in their own persons the penalty for their error.*

I also read from the book of Leviticus, Chap 18, Verse 22. *You shall not lie with a male as with a woman; it is an abomination.* With that, I slammed my Bible shut. The pledges were not horrified. The whole group of fourteen young faces stood silent and blinking. Their silence infuriated me. I left them to struggle with their own demons as I walked out the door announcing, "I'm no longer a part of this sin-filled organization!" Lynsey tried to talk with me, but I refused to listen. I spent that night at home, in my mother's house, and wondered if I ought to drop out of college altogether.

Instead of dropping out, the next day I took my shock and horror upstairs in the administration building to the offices of faculty in the religion department. I wandered into the office of Dr. Paul Blankenship. I had heard he was a good guy. I needed a good guy to help me sort through what I had just experienced.

"I just found out there are *lesbians*," I whispered the nasty word, "in the sorority I was pledging. And I let them know what an abomination they are. But somehow, I came away feeling like the bad guy, like I'm in the wrong. I feel confused."

"Sounds like you're trying to make sense of some things that are new to you."

"I mean I'm sure about what's right and what's wrong. I've got strong faith."

"What does your strong faith tell you about how others should be treated?"

"Well, with kindness and love, of course. Unless they are breaking God's rules. Then it's my duty as a Christian to call out the sin."

"You thought the lesbians were breaking God's rules?" He had his elbows on his desk.

"Yes." I couldn't believe there was any question about that. I wondered if I had stumbled upon the wrong religious man.

"Which rule?"

"The rule that says homosexuality is an abomination."

He reached behind him and picked up a Bible from his desk. "Can you show me where that is written as a rule?" He handed the Bible to me, and I took it, turning to Leviticus 18:22. I felt confident that I had made my point. "Paul, in writing to the Romans, says clearly that people who are having sex with people who are the same gender are exercising debased passions." Dr. Blankenship was kind. I could feel his genuine care about what was happening here. "But what if your interpretation of that scripture is wrong, rather than the lesbians in your sorority being wrong for what they are doing?"

"It's not my sorority any longer and how could I be wrong when it's written right there?"

"Tell me about your understanding of God's word."

"It's the truth, the life and the way." I knew I was right about that.

"Yes. But what if the truth, the life and the way is not just about that what is written but is about Jesus, the man, the one who ate with tax collectors, lepers and women, the one who spoke up for the poor, hungry, orphans, and widows? What if the word of God is more than something printed on paper or an ancient law? What if the word of God is Jesus, that spirit of kindness who lives in you and me and all Christians?

We are the hands and feet of Jesus in this world. I just wonder if you can imagine him, as you've been taught to imagine him, as a man who would condemn two people for loving each other. Because being homosexual is not just about the sexual act. It's about a natural attraction and a relationship that follows. The same sort of thing that heterosexual couples experience."

It seemed like a question was in all of that somewhere and I was not about to answer. The man had gone too far. My mind could not accept that this religion professor who should have known more about the Bible than I knew, was going to drop a bomb on me by suggesting I was wrong instead of those lesbians. I stood up and made my apologies. "I need to get to the language lab. Spanish, you know?" And I left Dr. Blankenship's office.

Little did I know that in thirty-five years I would find myself married to a woman and serving a church as their pastor. Looking back, I believe my fury and accusations were reactions to my own internal desires, desires I couldn't acknowledge. My reaction to the lesbians in my dorm room had little to do with religion and a lot to do with my refusal to accept myself. Years would go by before I settled into self-acceptance.

After the long Thanksgiving weekend, I moved in with another roommate, Connie Borslin. She didn't belong to a sorority, and she didn't mind my late-night returns when I came in after working in the theater. She had her life and her friends, and I had mine in the theater. Theater friends stick together. Everybody had a big need to be seen, to be heard, to express ourselves in a variety of voices. We worked out our neediness in and around the stage. I had a need to be seen underneath all the layers of masks I wore as a good Nazarene. The theater promised more to me than anything I had ever experienced. It seemed real, rather than a bunch of statements of belief. I didn't feel judged by my theater friends.

One Sunday I was working in the theater, helping to build a set for our children's theater event coming up. Suddenly I realized that it was time for church. In those days we went to church on Sunday morning and on Sunday night and Wednesday night for prayer meeting. It was time for church, and I was covered with paint and wearing shorts and an old t-shirt. I begged Joan, another member of the stage construction crew, for a ride to church. She laughed all the way, poking fun at me for needing to go to my mother's church. And I laughed with her. Maybe it was weird for me to go to church every time the doors were open, but that was what I had always done. I hurried into the sanctuary and walked up the center aisle to sit beside my mother. I heard whispers. As I scooted in next to my mother, I heard the hissing voice of Edna Gander, "Who do you think you are, coming to church dressed like that?" I felt shame wash over me. I stayed to the end of the service and my mother gave me a ride back to my dorm. But I never went back to my mother's church. Not once. Not ever. I was experiencing the theater, a community of people who really cared about me, who never hissed at me about my clothes. I decided I didn't need church. And just to prove I was serious about my changes; I started smoking cigarettes.

Every theater show has a cast party to mark the end of a good time. I started attending parties with my theater friends and I got interested in what the others were drinking, eating and smoking. I gently opted for a beer, or a glass of Blue Nun and I realized that I liked the feeling. It made me sway to the music. It made me laugh more easily. It erased my anxiety about food and calories.

After a performance of "The Physicists," we all crowded into the house that my brother, Edward, and his two roommates rented. I had been the go-between in setting up the plan. There seemed to be an unending supply of long neck beer being passed around. And a produce pan in the refrigerator was full of something pink they were calling "refrigerator punch." I drank several glasses of that sweet stuff. Then I stumbled into a bedroom and passed out.

I was sort of awakened by the weight of somebody on top of me. I woke up enough to mumble something and to struggle a little. I woke up enough to know who it was, Raymond Floyd, one of my brother's roommates, on top of me. But I passed out again. And I only aroused myself when the sun rose. I sat up to brush the bright light away. My head was spinning and starting to throb. I stood up and realized I had no pants on. And then I recognized the feeling. Things weren't right down there. I had been violated. Scrambling for my pants, which were tossed on the end of the bed, I got out of the house and sat on the front steps, realizing I had been raped. If only I hadn't drunk so much of that punch! I was a sinner, lost from God. I decided to walk home, to my mother's house, about two miles away. She would have a pot of coffee made.

"You look like something the cats drug in," she laughed.

I poured myself a cup of coffee and wished that I could tell my mother what had happened. But I knew she would blame me. I sipped my coffee and watched her as she ironed the wrinkles out of her husband's shirts.

One night I came back to my dorm room from play rehearsal, and I found Connie along with Lee Ann and Cindy sitting around in the dark. A lava lamp glowed on Connie's desk. They were smoking a tiny cigarette, passing it from one to the other. Connie jumped up and closed the door behind me. "All right. You caught us. Now you need to know that what we're doing is totally illegal. I mean we could go to jail for what we're doing. So, we need to hear you make a promise, let's hear you say you will not tell a soul. Got it?" Once again, I was the outsider. My roommate was smoking marijuana. I only knew the word because of an article I had read in the Herald of Holiness.

"You want some?"

"I might. What will it do for me?"

"It will make you relax and love listening to music. But let's have that promise." She waved her middle finger in my face.

"I promise and I'll try it."

We went out on the ball field and sat in the dugout where we passed a joint from hand to hand. I got the giggles, and we walked back to the dorm leaning on each other and singing, "This little light of mine; I'm gonna let it shine."

The next morning as Connie was brushing her hair and I was gathering my books for class, I asked, "What else is available for me to try?"

"What do you mean?"

"I mean, are there other feel-good drugs I could try?"

"There's some speed, black widows. And Arlo has some mescaline he's selling."

"What does it do for you, the mescaline?"

"It takes you on a psychedelic trip. People enjoy colors and music when they trip on mescaline."

"I want to try that. Can you get some for me?"

"Are you sure?" Connie seemed dubious. Only the day before I had seemed like such a goody two-shoes. But I was tired of being the one left out, the person from whom others had to keep secrets. I was tired of worrying constantly about my body weight and I wondered if a drug existed that could make me become my own best friend or not care at all.

That evening after dinner, Connie brought powdered mescaline to me. I swallowed the powder with a cola and went outside to sit on the front steps until my trip started. At first, I thought nothing unusual was going to happen but after an hour, the buildings on campus began to tilt and sway.

The trees nodded and waved their boughs at me. I felt the earth moving under my feet and it seemed to be calling on me to move too. I felt energized as I walked down Campbell Street, stopping by the duck pond where I sat on the bank and watched the ducks gliding effortlessly across the surface of the water. Cattails nodded. I appreciated the smell of wet earth and freshly mowed grass. Darkness covered me as I sat there, and I became aware of feeling thirsty. I got up and headed toward the Dairy Queen up the hill.

I stepped inside the door and felt assaulted by the fluorescent lights overhead. Other people were in line to order their ice cream treats and drinks. I waited my turn and as I waited, I noticed the faces around me. People had two sides to their faces, very distinct differences and I had never seen that before. I could see sadness in the eyes of one woman as she stood, holding the hand of her little boy. I also noticed that the man next to me was wearing a shirt that was too small for him. The buttons were bulging to the point where they might snap off at any minute. He stepped up to the window and accepted a huge ice cream cone dipped in chocolate. I saw a drip fall from his cone onto the counter and several flies landed on it. Suddenly I was overwhelmed by all that I was noticing, and I raced out the door. Taking a seat on a bench in front of the DQ, I took a deep breath. Closed my eyes. Just then a voice called my name. "Elaine?"

It was Lynsey, my old roommate and she was getting out of Brenda's car. "Are you all right?" she asked. Brenda sauntered over toward me, her hands in her pants pockets.

I couldn't find my voice. I simply stared at Lynsey.

"We're going in to get some ice cream. You want something?"

I shook my head and they both went inside. I sat, swinging my feet and wondering why I couldn't speak. I looked inside and caught Lynsey gesturing toward me and talking to Brenda.

"Let us give you a ride back to campus, ok?" Lynsey offered when they came out, licking their ice cream. I didn't argue because I couldn't speak.

Simply nodding, I followed them to Brenda's Mustang. I got in the back seat and watched the back of their heads as we rode up the hill and back to campus. I was lost in wonder, wondering how it could possibly be that these two women, who I had publicly accused of being sinful, an abomination in our midst, were now being kind and helpful toward me. I could see that they harbored no hate. They were licking their ice cream and trying to make small talk with me. But I had nothing to say. There was too much for me to wonder about and I couldn't find any words.

When the car stopped, I leaped out of the back seat and took off running. I ran to Harris Hall, the dorm for junior and senior women. I ran up to the third floor and straight to Sally Moretti's room. I had heard from others that Sally knew about psychedelic drugs and taking trips. I believed I would be safe if I could get to her.

Sally was the queen of our theater. She could act, direct, sing and play piano. We all thought she would soon become a star. She had put in a good word for me at Village Inn Pizza Parlor where she worked, and I got hired. We made pizza together and we made theater together. I adored her. She called me Little Chick.

So that night, the night of my first mescaline trip, I stood in the doorway of Sally's dorm room, and she looked up from the book she was reading. "What's happening, Little Chick?"

I looked at Sally's roommate, Cherry. Then back at Sally. Cherry took the hint and left the room. Alone, I managed to say, "Mescaline."

"Oh wow. You're tripping?" I nodded. "How's it going?" She closed her book and moved to sit on her bed, motioning for me to join her.

I sat down and let out a sigh. "I need to know."

"What do you need to know?"

"I need to know how it could be that sinners are kind, nice to me."

"Somebody was nice to you?"

"Yes. And I was cruel to them. But they were kind to me. And they don't even go to church or read their Bible. They're homosexual too. I told them…" I could hardly form the words, I felt so ashamed. "I told them they were going to hell for what I saw them doing. But they act as if it never happened."

Sally got dressed and we went outside to sit on the front steps of her dorm. We talked all night long. We were there to see the first rays of light when the sun came up. "God," I realized as dawn appeared, "is so much bigger than church. And goodness can be found in everyone." I also realized that Sally liked me as much as I liked her. We put speakers in the window of her dorm room and turned up the volume on Sally's record player. We played Carol King's song,

*You've got to get up every morning with a smile on your face and show the world all the love in your heart! Cause people gonna treat you better; you're gonna find, yes you will, that you're beautiful, you're beautiful, you're beautiful as you feel!*

# CHAPTER II

## I MIGHT BE A LESBIAN

When summer arrived, Sally went home to Pennsylvania and I was left, bereft, in Tennessee, working at the pizza parlor. I no longer felt comfortable at my mother's house. I was smoking cigarettes and drinking beer. My mother and her husband were disgusted by what they referred to as my spiritual dissipation. I didn't make enough money to cover rent on my own.

I went over to the campus to see Dr. Blankenship. "I need to decide something."

"What are you deciding?"

"I am realizing I'm in love.

Dr. Blankenship clapped his hands, grinning ear to ear. "Well, love is as good as it gets in this life."

"Yes, but she's a woman." I gave him a minute if he needed to react, but he seemed unfazed by my revelation.

"Are you in love together?" His eyebrows were raised, anticipating good news.

"I think she loves me too."

"Well, congratulations! How wonderful for both of you. What's her name?"

"Sally. Sally Moretti."

"Of course! I know Sally. A talented young woman. Smart too."

"But she left and went home to Pennsylvania. I can hardly breathe since she's gone. I need to go to Pennsylvania, too. Or I feel like I might fall apart."

"Well, let's avoid falling apart and, instead, let's celebrate the love. When do you plan to leave for Pennsylvania?"

"Tomorrow, by Greyhound Bus." I felt his enthusiasm as permission to beam happily.

"You might want to talk with your mother before you go. Ask her how she's feeling about your changes. You know, just to stay connected. She's very important to you, right?"

"Right."

I took my paycheck from the pizza parlor, cashed it, and asked my mother for a ride to the Greyhound Bus Station. "I can't be happy away from Sally, so I intend to follow her to Pennsylvania," I told my mother. I told my boss, Mr. Kilburn, I would be back in time for school to start again. But I didn't tell Sally that I was coming. I wanted to surprise her. My mother gave me a ride to the bus station and handed me two twenty-dollar bills.

"Honey, I really think you need to wear shoes on this trip," my mother sighed when she looked at me. My feet were bare; I was wearing a halter top and cut off blue jean short shorts. A leather hat with a wide brim topped off my look with a dangling racoon tail. I was eager to start my adventure.

"You know," my mother looked closely at my face, "it's just as well for you that your father died when he did. Because he was really at the end of his patience with you."

"He was?" I sat back down in the car and stared straight ahead, wondering about this revelation.

"Yes, he was. I mean, you were always so boisterous, loud. Not at all the kind of daughter he imagined having."

"Oh." There was nothing I could think of to say to that. "Thanks for the ride and the money, Mama."

"You behave yourself, now. Try to act like the good girl you were raised to be." She waved and shook her head as I got on the bus with a one-way ticket to Allentown, Pennsylvania.

I sat beside an older black woman. She had a shawl over her shoulders and was staring out the window as I settled in the seat beside her. Once we got out on the highway, she introduced herself. "I'm Trudy, Trudy Richardson." She smiled a wide grin and reached in a shopping bag, pulling out a bottle of whiskey. "Want some?" When I grinned and nodded, she pulled a plastic cup from her bag and handed it to me. She poured coffee from a thermos and then she poured whiskey on top of that. Chuckling a deep, throaty sound, she sat back and settled herself, drinking from the lid of her thermos. She talked and I listened as the bus rolled over the highway. I learned every detail about Trudy's life and her family. She was headed to Virginia to see her son and I was sorry to say goodbye to her when she got off the bus.

The Allentown bus station was busy. I asked the woman at the ticket counter, "How many miles to Fullerton?"

"It's about nine miles from here."

"Is there a bus that would take me there?"

"No, no bus. You'll need a taxi if no one plans to pick you up."

I sighed and looked around. I didn't want to spend what was left of my money on a taxi ride and I wasn't sure I even had enough to cover the cost of a taxi. I'd never ridden in a taxi and had no idea how much it would cost. I walked outside, just to get a breath of fresh air and to see the city. A deep gray sky loomed over me as I leaned on a telephone pole and pondered what to do next. A black Fleetwood Cadillac drove by, going slowly enough for me to get a good look at the two older men in the front seat. They were looking at me too.

I considered calling Sally for a ride but that would spoil the surprise. The black Cadillac rolled by a second time and this time the car stopped. The window rolled down and one of the elderly gentlemen asked, "Do you need a ride?"

"I do. I need to get to Fullerton."

He stepped out of the car and gestured for me to get in. "Not a problem." I sat between the two men in the front seat. "Where in Fullerton are you going?" the driver asked.

I gave them Sally's address. "It's my girlfriend's house. We've been together at school, and I miss her. I'm surprising her."

"What's your girlfriend's name?"

"Sally Moretti."

"Moretti. I know a Tony Moretti."

"That's her uncle. Uncle Tony has been in prison but he's out now. She's told me all about her family."

"Right. I remember when Tony's case went to court. Who is Sally's dad?"

"Her dad is John, John Moretti."

"Oh yes. A good man. How long will you be visiting Sally?"

"Maybe the rest of the summer. We'll see."

"So, you and Sally are in school together?"

"Yes. We're both theater majors. Sally is an amazing actress."

"Do you act?"

"I do. I'm not as talented as Sally, and I don't have as much experience on stage as she has. But I'm learning."

The two men looked at each other and the driver spoke. "You know, we have connections in the city. We can hook you up with a man who works for MGM studios. Would you like to meet him? He might be able to get you on television or in a movie. Just depends on what's happening around here now. You interested?"

"Yes." It was all happening so fast. I was closer to Sally than I'd been in weeks and already there were good things coming my way. "I would love to meet this man. What's his name?"

"His name is Mark Hampson, and we'll get him to give you a call in the next day or so. Is that ok with you? What's Sally's phone number?"

Mrs. Moretti was the only person at home when we arrived. She was in the middle of cooking dinner and had a dish towel tossed over her shoulder as she answered the door. "Come in! Come in!" She welcomed all three of us and scurried about, leading us out to the den where we sat, and she offered us drinks.

The two men chatted with Sally's mother, letting her know that they knew the family as we all sipped cold beer. I looked around, imagining Sally in this place and longing to see her. "Oh," Mrs. Moretti assured me, "she'll be home soon. She went into Bethlehem to talk to her friend, John Shifter. He has a shop in town and Sally hopes he'll hire her for the summer. He makes rings and things with silver. And he makes leather purses and belts. She'll tell you all about it when she

72

gets here. Boy! She is going to be really surprised when she gets home."

And she was. She was surprised and very happy to see me.

We both got hired at John's Silver Shop in Bethlehem, working nine to five Tuesday through Saturday.

Mark Hampson called me a week after my arrival. "I understand you're an actress?"

"I am."

"Let's have lunch, how about it, and you can tell me about yourself and what you dream of doing. I've got some ideas that might make your dreams come true."

He picked me up at John's Silver Shop. "Don't worry, Sally," I reassured her when she cautioned me about going off with a stranger. I hopped into Mark's car. "He's a friend of your family."

We ate lunch at McDonald's and Mark seemed in a hurry to finish eating as I told him about my studies at college.

"Let's go for a ride and I'll give my friend at MGM a call. OK?"

We stopped at a Howard Johnson's motel and restaurant. "Just a minute," Mark said as he jumped out of the car and went into the office. I wondered if his MGM friend worked at the motel. I was sure we weren't going to go into the restaurant to eat again. Mark returned with a key in his hand.

"Let's relax a bit and I'll call my friend from our room."

I wanted so badly to be discovered as an actress, I started trembling and I wasn't sure if my sudden anxiety was from excitement or fear. I wondered if I ought to call Sally, but I didn't know the number for the silver shop. I said nothing, following Mark into the room. He flopped on the bed and said, "There's no need to hurry. Let's just enjoy each other for a while. I can make the call for you any time. Why don't you take those clothes off and let me see what you've got to offer MGM?" He unfastened his belt and unzipped his pants.

I scurried into the bathroom and locked the door. I touched a towel hanging on the rack and then grasped it tightly. "Take me back to the silver shop." I said it once and then I repeated it with all the force my dry throat would allow. "Take me back to the silver shop."

"Get back out here. I'm not going to hurt you."

"Take me back to the silver shop right now."

He came to the bathroom door. "Get your sweet ass out here, honey. We're just going to have some fun and then I'm going to call my friends at MGM studio and make your dreams come true."

"No. I just want to go back to the silver shop."

I was staring at the bathroom wall and willing myself back to the shop, back to the safety of Sally.

"Well," his voice took on fury. "Get the goddamn fuck out of there, you stupid bitch. What did you think was going to happen here?" I heard his belt buckle rattle, and my trembling increased. "Get out here, now."

I came out and walked to the door, not looking at the man, just imagining Sally's face and her arms that would hold me closely when I got back to the shop.

We got into Mark's car, and he drove like an angry man, as I slid around on his leather seats. He stopped at a warehouse and went inside. I wondered if I ought to get out and run, but I had no idea where we were. Then he came back out and drove me into town where he stopped behind the shop. I got out and ran, relieved to be alive and free to run from the man, his anger and his big car.

The next evening, I was at the table eating dinner with the Moretti family. John was home from his office job at Bethlehem Steel. Mrs. Moretti always had dinner ready when he got home. We were having roast lamb, rice, broccoli and dinner rolls when the black Fleetwood pulled into the driveway. The two men who had picked me up in Allentown got out of the car and came to the front door.

I got up and went quickly to meet them, afraid that they might tell Sally's parents about the day before. I was afraid Mr. and Mrs. Moretti might think I was the kind of girl who went to motel rooms with men. Shame flew all over me.

"Hi, sweetheart." The men smiled when I opened the door. "We understand things didn't go so well with you and Mark yesterday. Come on out to the car. We brought a little something to say how sorry we are." I knew the whole family was listening, so I stepped outside and followed them to the car where the one man opened the back door and pointed to two gifts wrapped and ribboned. "We think these dresses will fit you nicely. We had to guess about the size, but we think you'll look lovely in both."

"I don't want a dress of any size, not from you," I said and crossed my arms across my chest.

Mr. Moretti came outside and walked over to me. "What's going on here?"

"These men are offering gifts to me, and I don't want them," I said.

"This young lady is a guest in my home," Mr. Moretti was firm. "And I think the two of you had best take your gifts and leave her alone."

"Certainly, John," the men didn't waste any time getting into the car and leaving.

"Let's finish our dinner," Mr. Moretti put his arm around my waist and guided me up the walk to the house. "We've got chocolate pie for dessert."

No one at the table asked me any questions. We ate pie in silence.

The Moretti family belonged to the Moravian Church in Bethlehem. I attended Sunday school and church with them. Then Sally and I dropped acid and tripped together on Sunday afternoons. We swam in their pool and walked the family dog along the Erie Canal. Sally's younger sister, Andrea, sometimes joined us on our walks and when we went shopping. A tight-knit extended family, the Morretti's were fun to be with. Sally's grandmother was my favorite. She did her best to fatten me up that summer.

Both of us got our jobs back at Village Inn when we returned to Tennessee, and we rented an apartment near campus. Dorm life had been too confining. Sally decorated our place and my brother, Edward, loaned us his car when he left town with a group of guys heading to Colorado to do construction work. We had everything we needed. Our friends quickly learned where to find us and we became the safe place to hang out, the safe place to get high. Our apartment was full of color, music, and food. Sally was an artist, a musician, and an excellent cook. She baked bread on Saturdays and the house smelled like hospitality. We listened to Laura Nyro, Judy Collins, Joni Mitchell, Aretha Franklin, Janis Joplin, the Beatles, Crosby, Stills and Nash. We dropped acid or mescaline every Tuesday afternoon and tripped with our friends. It was a magical time. The magic took over my thinking and I dropped out of school despite Sally's disapproval. School wasn't feeding my soul. I wanted more time to listen to music, ride my bike and be with Sally at home and at the pizza parlor.

I loved Sally more than I had ever loved anyone. I wanted her happiness; I craved the sound of her full-throated laugh. But the world brought her down. She protested the Viet Nam War, racism and any kind of discrimination or human oppression. She was a fighter, a poet and a lover of justice. But some days she seemed depressed by the struggle. One day she was taking a bath and feeling low.

"What's the matter, Sally?" I sat on the tub beside her and scrubbed her back.

"So much is the matter, Little Chick. And on top of the major problems in this world, we are about to be out of cigarettes. And pay day is not until Friday."

I left Sally in the tub, grabbed one of her big leather bags, got on my bicycle, and rode over to Liberty Grocery where I wandered around, looking at things on the shelves. When I thought no one was looking, I stuck two cartons of cigarettes, Marlboros for me and Kools for Sally, in my bag. Then I walked to the front of the store, picked up an Almond Joy bar and stood in the check-out line. Suddenly a hand grabbed my upper arm and a man's voice growled, "What's in your bag, girlie?" I peed my pants as I turned to face the store manager. "Come with me," he demanded. "I've seen you in here before with that bag and I'm not letting you get away this time." I was dragged to the manager's office where he called the police.

"You don't want to call the police on me!" I talked fast and furiously as I dropped the two cartons of cigarettes on his desktop. "My mother is a teacher, and my stepfather is a preacher here in town! It will kill them to know what I've done. I promise you I'll never ever steal again if you'll just let me go. I swear to God I won't steal from this store or anybody ever again."

"All right. I'll let you go." I started crying when I realized his mercy on me. "But I don't want to ever see your face or that bag in this store again. You hear me?"

When the man let go of my arm, I raced to the door of the store. As I exited, a police officer entered the store. I got on my bike and rode with a fury toward home. Sally was still sitting in the tub, soaking. "Where'd you go?"

"Nowhere, just rode my bike around." My heart was pounding so hard I could barely speak.

"What are you doing out there?" Sally called.

"I'm just getting ready to go over to campus and bum some cigarettes for us," I answered as I put on dry pants. I walked down to campus and bummed several cigarettes from a friend, Lorenzo, and brought them back to Sally.

After two years of being with Sally, I began to wonder if I might be a lesbian. Sally had graduated. We were no longer college kids but two working women. I hadn't thought of myself or Sally as lesbians. We were simply two people deeply in love. Our love making was sweet and passionate. I never wondered if I might be attracted to any other woman. I wasn't like that. Being with Sally seemed like the right place for me. But by the second summer, when we were both working long hours, the romance of our lives wore thin. Some of our closest friends had graduated from college and many of them had moved away. There was no time for theater or tripping. I imagined my future tossing pizzas and pouring beer for rowdy customers. I began to feel lost, and I blamed it on being in love with a woman.

# MY TRUE LOVE SANG AT
# MY WEDDING

I told Sally I didn't love her anymore but what I should have said was, "I am afraid of giving my life to our love."

Sally asked me where the love had gone and I had no answer for her. I was nineteen with almost no self-awareness. I only knew that something in me was growing ashamed of a love that had to remain our secret. We couldn't kiss at work when the spirit moved us to express our love. We had to pretend with Sally's parents and extended family that we were just good friends. The secrecy inspired my shame.

I moved home to Mom's place. I went back to college for a semester. Sally moved home to Pennsylvania. Instead of grieving the loss of a beautiful relationship, I immediately started looking for another love object, preferably a guy. I was in a hurry to look normal.

Doug Miller, a friend and a regular visitor to our apartment, got high with me after Sally left town. He took me to a David Bowie concert in Memphis. A nice guy, a poet and a folksinger, Doug drove his mother's car, and he had no regular job although he had graduated from college. On the way home from Memphis, I scooted closer and closer to Doug's side.

The stick shift kept my legs on my side of the car. But my lips found his neck and I blew on it. And my hand touched his inner thigh. We had sex in the back seat of his mother's car. This passed for normal, at least in my mind.

We put our thumbs out and hitched a series of rides to Dallas where we spent a summer living with Doug's friend, Bill. Doug got a job working for The Iconoclast, an underground newspaper, and I got a job at Wayne's Lone Star Donuts. When Doug said, "I think we should get married," I agreed. Family and friends tried to talk me out of the marriage. But I wasn't listening.

The first time I saw Doug arrested we were still in Dallas and Doug was delivering papers to downtown boxes and businesses. The cops pulled us over and pulled Doug out of the car. They handcuffed him and Doug hollered at me, "Call Bill!" I found a pay phone and called Bill who brought a friend with him to drive our Oldsmobile back to Bill's place. I couldn't drive; I had never learned to drive and was not at all interested in learning. It seemed like more responsibility than I could handle. Bill provided the money to get Doug out of jail. When I asked what had happened, Doug said he had some outstanding parking tickets that needed to be paid.

We left Dallas and returned to Tennessee, where we moved in with Doug's mother and made plans to be married.

We set the date for August 25, 1973, and reserved the college campus chapel. My mother made the wedding gown, a simple white cotton dress, and I wore a garland of daisies in my hair. Dr. Gene Davenport agreed to officiate. He asked to meet with us prior to the ceremony. "Your mother's opinion of you seems to be important in your mind," he observed, as we nibbled on cookies and sipped tea in his office.

Doug interjected, "Her mother is highly critical of Elaine. When we announced we were getting married, her mother asked me if I have a playpen big enough to hold her."

The rehearsal dinner was in the backyard of Doug's mother's house. We had food that I had requested…ham, asparagus casserole, grits casserole, green beans, sliced tomatoes, pickles, biscuits, and coconut cake. It was a feast served on picnic tables covered with red and white checked tablecloths. Both of our families were there along with Sally, who I had invited to sing at my wedding and Sandy Adams, who I had always promised that if I were to get married, she would be my maid of honor.

After the rehearsal dinner my brother, Eric, invited several of us to join him in his hotel room for drinks. Doug's best man, Kenny McGough, joined us there along with Doug's brothers, Mike and Jim, and my brothers, Eugene, and Edward. Everyone crowded into the hotel room. We drank several bottles of wine, and my brothers became belligerent. Eugene threatened to beat Kenny's ass, accusing him of being a "no-good pothead." A punch was thrown, and Kenny's eye was blackened. Just before we exited the room, Eugene pulled me into the bathroom and asked, "Have you told this guy that you can't have children? Because that's something a man needs to know before he marries you. Have you had a period in the last year or so?"

"No. I don't have periods." I was shocked and embarrassed by my brother's sudden interest in my intimate life. I had no idea he cared about me since we had hardly spoken in years. Now, the night before my wedding, he was concerned about my menstrual cycle. I wanted out of the bathroom, but Eugene blocked the door.

"What the hell, Elaine! Are you leading this poor guy into something he's going to regret?"

"Let me out," I shoved him. And he shoved me back, knocking me against the wall.

"You've turned into a total disappointment to our mother. I hope you know that. If you don't tell that guy about how sick you are, then I'll tell him myself." Eugene was drunk; his words were slurring.

"Ok. I'll tell him. Just let me out." I found Doug, Kenny, and Doug's brothers already outside, waiting for me by the Oldsmobile. The car was a wedding gift from Doug's mother. We drove the others home and then we parked and smoked a joint. "You know I don't have periods, right? That's why we don't use protection. Right?" Doug nodded. "And that's all right with you that I can't get pregnant?" He pulled on the joint and held the smoke in his lungs.

When he exhaled, he said, "Don't think twice. It's all right."

The next day, at our wedding, I was trembling so violently that my bouquet shook. My teeth were chattering as the music played, and I stood in the back of the chapel with my mother. I had no one to walk me down the long aisle. Sandy was waiting for me, standing by the preacher. Doug and Bill, his best man, looked up the aisle, waiting. I was afraid I couldn't do it. That's when my mother grabbed my arm and pulled me aside, shoving me up against the wall. "Listen to me," she demanded. "You don't have to do this. You don't have to marry this guy if you're not ready. You can walk out that door right now and I'll take care of the rest."

I heard her words while Sally started singing, *What I'll give you since you asked is all my time together. Take the rugged sunny days, the warm and rocky weather. Take the roads that I have walked along, looking for tomorrow's time, peace of mind.* I walked shakily down the aisle and took Doug's hand. I was afraid of backing out, afraid of how much I still loved Sally. Vows were spoken and the service went on as planned.

After the reception, Doug and I drove to the apartment my mother had secured for us, paying four months' rent as a wedding gift. Doug settled himself on the couch and turned on the television, watching a football game. I took off my wedding dress and hung it behind our bedroom door. Doug hollered, "Make me a couple hotdogs, will you?" We had no money for a honeymoon.

The next morning, I was awakened early by a knock on our door. It was Sandy. She was still dressed in her bride's-maid gown and wearing her floppy hat. "Your brother!" she exclaimed as I opened the door for her. "Eric is amazing!" She had slept with my brother, and she said, "I'm in love!" Sandy's feelings for Eric were so intense that she got a job working as a waitress with me at Jerry's Restaurant. She seemed confident that Eric, who lived in Murfreesboro at the time, would invite her to live with him. He was in between wives, having divorced his first wife and not yet married to his second wife. Sandy lived with us for a month and, when Eric returned none of her calls, she went back home to California.

The second time Doug was arrested, the sheriff was waiting in our driveway with a warrant when we drove home from work. Doug saw the sheriff's car in the driveway and instead of pulling in, he floored the accelerator and tried to outrun the sheriff who was immediately in pursuit. Again, Doug was handcuffed and taken to jail. The warrant for that arrest was the result of his having written checks that were not covered by money in the bank. Doug's mother posted bond, and she covered the amount of the outstanding checks. We learned that Doug was gambling, betting on games and races, anything that might win or lose.

I began to think I had made another bad decision, and I wondered how I could manage my life better. I lived with the constant secret of vomiting my food and the fear that I would be blamed for some catastrophe. Doug never noticed. He had his mind on his own secrets. But I ate enough and digested enough to start having periods, although irregularly. My annual pap smear in 1974 showed precancerous cells on my cervix, so I had surgery, a scraping of the cervix.

# HAVING A BABY

T he idea of having a baby appealed to me. "A baby," I tried to convince Doug to see things my way, "would give our life focus and we could find our own place, move out of your mother's house. We could become a family." A baby, I hoped, would make me feel needed and would make Doug stop gambling. It was a lot to put on a baby, but that was how I was thinking at the time. Doug didn't object to the idea of our having a baby, so we started working on making that happen. I saw the obstetrician and he gave me three small pills, some kind of hormone. "Take one of these daily for the next three days," he said. In January, 1976, I learned I was pregnant.

Being pregnant released me from my fear of food. I ate well while I carried Jennifer, and I had no urge to vomit what I ate. I found myself intrigued with the way my body grew larger. It wasn't that I was getting fat and sloppy; rather, I was becoming a mother. My body became a household for new life. My emotions adjusted to the changes as my body adjusted to her development inside me. I gained forty pounds during the pregnancy. I stopped smoking and I stopped drinking beer. I walked four miles a day to stay in shape. I felt the sacredness of life and I remembered the benefits of fostering my faith. I began to journal every day, and I spent time in prayer.

Becoming a mother became a holy endeavor, a privilege, and a thing of great beauty. I fed my body, and I fed my soul while the baby grew.

Eleven days after my 24th birthday, I cleaned the house, washed the car and did four loads of laundry. I sang while I folded sheets and shirts. As we sat at the dinner table, eating pork chops, English peas and mashed potatoes, Doug's mother asked me, "How long have you been having those contractions?" She could see my shirt rising.

"I don't know what you're talking about." I felt nothing. But Betty, who was a nurse anesthetist, had had years of experience with pregnant women in labor and during delivery. She finished her dinner and got dressed.

"Let's get to the hospital now," she said. "Let's don't wait until you feel pain."

"But Doug isn't home," I argued. It seemed unwise to go to the hospital without him.

"Where is he?" Betty asked and when I shrugged, we both knew he was out gambling. He played pinball machines for hours and cashed in on his winnings. "We're not waiting on him."

My mother-in-law sat beside me in the hospital labor room and encouraged me. "Your mother would be so proud of you if she were here," she said. Betty knew all the staff in the labor and delivery unit and saw to it that I got the care I needed. I had an epidural and off we went to the delivery room where Betty held my hand as Jennifer came into the world. She weighed six pounds and eight ounces. She was healthy and beautiful. I fell asleep immediately after her birth.

When I woke up in the hospital room, Doug was sitting beside my bed and the nurse was there, handing me our baby. I was amazed at how perfect she was, her perfect nose and ears, her fingers and toes, her little mouth was lovely, and I was taken by how sweet her hair looked. She was hungry and rooted for my breast. I had not been warned about the cramps that came with the first few days of breastfeeding. I did my best to feed her, and the nurse reassured me that the awful abdominal cramping was normal and would not last forever.

When family and friends came to visit us in the hospital, I put on a bathrobe and walked them down the hall to the glassed-in nursery where they could view our new baby. She was in a bassinet in a row with other babies and I felt sorry for the other mothers and their family and friends. It was obvious to me that our baby was the most beautiful baby in the nursery.

The second afternoon of my postpartum stay in the hospital, I began to cry. I had no idea it was going to happen and no way to stop the sobbing. I asked for a bath and the nurse showed me to the tub room where I ran a tub full of hot water. I soaked in the hot water and cried until the water cooled down. Then I let the water out and poured another tub full of hot water. I sobbed, all alone and confused about my sudden overwhelming sadness.

The fourth morning of my hospital stay, Doug came to pick us up. Our car was so old that the floorboard had holes in it. The pavement was visible as we rode toward the trailer that was our new home at Farmer's Trailer Park. I held our new baby and carried her into the house. Doug's mother was there to greet us. She had cleaned our trailer from top to bottom while I was in the hospital. The yellow bassinet that I had painted was in our bedroom. I put Jennifer into her bed and welcomed Kenny McGough at the front door. A photographer, Kenny took pictures of us with our new baby.

That night I worked on breastfeeding and took a shower in our new home. Doug went to work at his job as a short-order cook. But he came home early. "They fired me," he explained. He had been caught smoking a joint outside the truck stop and he lost his job. "It's fine," he said. "I can watch Jennifer while you're at work."

I continued to work as a waitress at Jerry's Restaurant, working the night shift. Doug brought Jennifer to me early each morning when he picked me up from work. There were times, at the end of my shift, when milk oozed from my breasts, ran down my sides and dripped into my shoes. I had an abundance of milk for our little girl, and as we rode home, I was relieved by her hungry sucking. I had to cover the breast she wasn't sucking from with a doubled-over diaper to keep it from squirting into the dashboard of our old car.

Without the assistance of Doug's mother, we would have lost our trailer home. Betty was determined to support us; she gave us rent money and she adored her grandchild, caring for her whenever Doug went out for the night. My mother and Jim came by to meet the baby when she was a few weeks old. They had moved to Dickson, Tennessee when I first got pregnant, so it was a two-hour drive from their house to our new place. I watched them leaning over the bassinet and wondered what kind of relationship my daughter would have with them. I knew I would not let her be a Nazarene or go to camp with her grandparents.

My depression deepened. I didn't want my little girl to grow up with a gambling father and a waitress for a mother. I wanted more for her and more for me. I resented how much help we needed from Doug's mother. I returned to smoking, drinking, and vomiting, looking for a way to feel in control. When Jennifer was a year old, I applied for financial aid to attend nursing school at Union University in Jackson. As a nurse I could pay our rent by myself, no matter what Doug did with his time. I also went to the obstetrician and asked to have my tubes tied so we wouldn't have the added cost of another child while I did what I could to become financially independent.

"You're too young to have your tubes tied," Dr. Clark objected.

"They're my tubes and I want them tied," I insisted. The surgery was scheduled and done. I breathed a sigh of relief.

# A Suicide Jogs My Memory

I was awarded a Pell Grant that paid for my tuition, my textbooks, and my supplies so that I could go to nursing school. It was a decision I made based largely on how kind and helpful the nurses had been to me when Jennifer was born. I wanted to assist people in the same way. I imagined myself helping people from the bed to the bathroom and educating them about their conditions. I didn't realize how challenging some aspects of nursing would be for me, like giving shots and starting intravenous infusions. My mother-in-law was a big help to me as I went through my training. In May of 1979, I graduated from nursing school with an associate degree. I went to Nashville to take my state board exams and became a registered nurse, working at Jackson Madison County Hospital as charge nurse on the sixth-floor psychiatric unit. I felt a particular connection to the suicidal and schizophrenic patients. I got to know them well and I got to know their families too.

Mrs. Jersey was a repeat patient on our unit. She was determined to kill herself. She had overdosed on pills and survived when her stomach was pumped. She tried to hang herself and was rescued by her husband. And then she stopped eating in an effort to starve herself to death. When she was admitted for the third hospitalization on our unit, her husband was worn out with caring for his wife, and Mrs. Jersey's adult children were traumatized by their mother's chronic depression and suicide attempts. I cared for all of them as best I could.

One night, while I was reporting to the night shift nurses, an aide came to the nurses' station and said, "Mrs. Jersey wants to see you."

I went down to her room and asked, "What do you need?" She didn't answer but she took my hand and squeezed it. She seemed so restless and agitated. I gave her a shot of Haldol, as ordered for agitation. And then I returned to the nurses' station and gave report. I charted my notes for my shift and went home.

At 6:00 the following morning I was awakened by the phone ringing. It was Kay, the night nurse to whom I had given the report. "Mrs. Jersey jumped out the window," she told me.

"What?"

"She pushed herself out that window and fell to the ground."

"How?"

"We don't know how. I just knew you would want to know. She's gone, Elaine. That fall shattered every bone in her tiny body."

Mrs. Jersey's suicide took a toll on my confidence as a nurse. It made no sense, but I felt somehow responsible as if that shot of Haldol had given the woman just the right amount of gumption to find a way to finally end her life. I went back over to campus and went upstairs to the religion department where Dr. Blankenship seemed happy to see me. I needed a listening ear. I asked Dr. Blankenship if he had time to listen to a long story, a terrible story about an incident that happened to me as a small child. "I feel like my life got off to a bad start and I can't seem to turn things around. I feel like I cause problems everywhere I go." I began to cry, and Dr Blankenship got up and closed his office door.

"Take your time. I'm listening," he said.

I told him about a black boy. A black boy who came from the row of six tin-roof shanties across the field from my childhood home in Gainesville. The shanties were on Second Street a place we called *Nigger Town*. My mother claimed, "We don't use *that* word in this house." But we did. I knew the word when the black boy and I met each other face to face. I knew not to use the word in front of him. We only used that language among our own kind. I was four when I met that boy and, my best guess, the black boy was probably fourteen.

I went across the field, hoping to attract a playmate, even though I had been told not to go over there. "Something terrible happened over there," I sobbed, "and I'm not sure I even want to know what happened."

Dr. Blankenship gave me time to cry and then he suggested that I drive to Dickson. "Go see your mother and ask her what happened in the field that day. It might be something she wants to talk about with you and she's just waiting for you to bring it up."

I took his suggestion and drove the two-hour drive from my home in Jackson, to see my mother and to engage her in conversation. I dreaded the moment when I would tell her what was on my mind. I was remembering enough of the experience with that black boy, enough to inform me that Mama wasn't going to be happy about my bringing it up. I halfway hoped she would tell me I was imagining things.

She was in her greenhouse, watering plants when I arrived. "Well, hello! What brings you over here today?" Always slim, my mother never weighed over a hundred pounds. She was proud of how limber her body was. She liked to sit on the floor and pull her ankles up behind her neck. "Can you do this?" she'd laugh, knowing the answer and relishing her physical superiority. I took a deep breath as she set down her watering can.

"I just wanted to see you. I have something I want to ask you about."

She said, "Well, ask away," as she carried the watering can to the faucet.

"I am wondering about a memory I have…" I wandered among her elephant ears and other tropical plants before continuing. "…about a black boy in the field across the street from us in Gainesville. Did Daddy and Eric go over there with Carl Reagan and…"

She whirled around, sloshing water across the floor. "Young lady! You were told to forget that!"

"So, it's true? Did they beat that boy up?"

"You listen to me. If you need to go around remembering things, you remember this: Carl Reagan was a terrible racist."

"What was the boy's name, Mama? I need to know his name."

"Well for goodness' sake! I have no idea what his name was. I wasn't involved."

"Involved! You were involved. I was your child!"

"Look. If the only reason you came over here today was to stir up trouble from the past, you can get in that car of yours and drive yourself back home. I don't have to put up with this nonsense. And if you need to blame somebody, you blame the Reagans."

I drove home crying. My tears came from a mixture of emotions. While it was painful to be dismissed by my mother, there was something gratifying about learning my memory was valid. The issue for my exploration was no longer *did it happen?* Instead, I worked on healing the hurt that came from being dismissed as a daughter and sister, and the pain of realizing my own family members were involved in a racist act of violence and injustice. I worked on transferring the shame that had landed on my shoulders and putting it where it belonged. "The truth is," I told Dr. Blankenship on my next visit, "my family did some horrible things to a poor black boy, and I seem to be the only one who feels badly about it." I told Dr. Blankenship the whole story.

I was a lonely, wounded and bored four-year-old, sitting on the front steps of our house, shaded by the giant live oak at the end of the sidewalk. Spanish moss was tossed by a breeze. The year was 1956. I picked up acorns and rolled them around in my hand. Edward had gone off to school and that left me with no one to play with. My two older brothers, Eric and Eugene, were in high school. They played instruments in the school band. Eugene played trumpet and Eric played trombone. They had girlfriends and cars to drive around. They both had jobs, their way to make money for dates and buying polish and gas for their precious Chevrolets. I tossed acorns toward the parked cars in front of our house. I got up and walked closer to the cars, aiming for the windshields. That's when I noticed those other kids. They were across the field, and they were laughing, chasing each other round and round one of those tin roof shanties. I hopped up and down, hoping one of those children would see me. When it became clear that I was not being noticed, I scooted out past the cars and climbed up on the back bumper of a Cadillac. I waved my arms, but those children were too busy having fun to see me.

"Mama! Mama!" I found her typing in her office. "Can I go across the field and play?" She was typing the church newsletter, carefully adjusting a mimeograph sheet. Her fingers were black from spreading ink on the barrel of the mimeograph machine.

"Don't bother me, Elaine. I'm busy."

"Mama! Look! There are children over there! Can I go over there and play?"

"What?" She raised her face to look at me and she put her glasses on. "Oh. No. Now run along. I've got work to do."

"But Mama! Why can't I go over there?"

She stopped typing and turned around so rapidly; I stepped back. "Because I said so and because it will just cause trouble."

"Trouble? What kind of trouble?"

With an exasperated sigh, "I do not have time to explain everything to you, young lady. Now go outside and let me get this done before time to fix your father's lunch."

I went next door to the church where my daddy was in his study. "Daddy! Daddy! Can I go across the field and play? There are children over there."

"What's that?" He was sitting at his desk in his office. He looked up from a book as I rushed in to see him. My daddy was handsome; I knew that for sure. Tall, with thick gray hair and a winning smile that suggested playfulness. He had a wonderful laugh. He liked to play tennis and he dabbled in golf. People liked my daddy. He had friends all over town, not just in the church. All of my friends were at church so the only time I got to play with my friends was Sunday afternoons.

I went home with Dian or Debbie. We had Sunday dinner with the family and then we took off playing. It was a Sunday treat. Dian had three sisters and no older brothers, so we felt safe at her house. There were times, during the week, when I could convince my daddy to take me over to a friend's house to play. I approached him with hope in my heart.

"I see children playing and having fun across the field. And I want to have fun too."

Daddy got up and looked out the window. "No. You can't go over there."

"Why not?"

"Because those children are negroes, and they have their own friends to play with." He sat back down and folded his hands neatly on top of his book.

"Their own friends? Well, do they go to school with the boys?"

"No. They have their own school, Lincoln Elementary."

"Their own school? Well, what about church? How come they don't come over here for church, living right there?"

"Because they have their own church and that's the way they like it. Now, run along. I've got a sermon to write." He waved me away and looked at the book on his desk.

Stomping back to the front steps, I stood and watched those children playing. Then I went inside and got my doll, Betsy, a doll blanket, and a broom. And I went halfway across that empty field, to a concrete foundation where I laid Betsy on her blanket and began sweeping pine needles away. "Softly and tenderly, Jesus is calling," I sang as I watched the activity over at those shanties.

A black boy rode by on his bicycle, and I waved. He was too big for playing dolls. "Calling for you and for me…"

The same boy rode by again, making wide circles around me. We eyed each other. I wondered why he wasn't in school.

The third time that black boy rode by, he stopped. Rolled his bike toward me. He didn't look right. His eyes were funny. A strand of drool hung from his lower lip and sparkled in the sunlight. His shoes were torn. I could see his toes. They looked like dusty peanuts. "You got a little sister, might like to play with me? Why are you looking at me that way?"

"You want some money?" He thrust both his hands down in his overall pockets.

"No! I do not want any money! Not from a retard like you!"

At that, the boy dropped his bike and ran toward me. I dropped my broom and left Betsy lying on the ground as I ran like crazy for home. "Whooee!" I slammed the front door behind me and flopped on the couch, huffing and puffing.

My daddy was home and thumbing through the day's mail. "What's got you so out of breath?"

"Big black boy. He was chasing me! Scared me half to death!"

"What black boy?" He bellowed, his face like flint toward the front window.

"Uh," his fury set me upright and alert, "a big black boy from over there," I pointed, "riding on a beat-up black bicycle, looked like a retard to me."

"You go to your room!" When I didn't move immediately, he hollered, "Now!"

I went to my room. I heard my daddy on the telephone. He was calling Carl Reagan, a police officer in our church. Pretty soon, Carl pulled up in our driveway in his police car. My oldest brother, Eric, came home from school early and I saw the three of them…Daddy, Eric and Carl get in the police car and back out the driveway. I watched as they rode around Second Street to that row of tin roof shanties. All the children were now out of sight. The police car stopped in front of a shanty where the beat-up black bike was leaned against the concrete block steps.

They all got out of the car. Carl jumped up on the porch and hammered his fists on the door. A woman came to the door. She was round and wearing an apron, carrying a dish towel. Carl pushed her out the way and went inside. Then he came out, dragging that black boy. Threw him off the porch and on the ground. That's when my brother, Eric, ran up in the yard and started kicking the boy. Kicking and kicking. Carl pulled out his billy-stick and started hitting the boy. The boy raised his hand up, as if to shield his face, and Carl lifted his arm and swung down hard. Then the boy was still. Carl and Eric dragged the boy across the ground and threw him in the backseat of the police car. That woman was still standing on the porch, holding her arms up in the air and shouting, "Oh Lord! Oh Lord!"

My daddy was standing on the sidewalk, looking this way and that. Eric started walking across the field, heading home. I watched as Daddy got in Carl's police car and they drove away.

I ran back to my room and pushed the toy box out of my way so I could hide in my closet. I heard my mama on the telephone. "Yes. Well, they took him downtown to the city jail. I know. I know. None of this would have happened if Elaine weren't so friendly."

Eric walked by my bedroom door and tossed Betsy on the floor by my bed. "There's your doll, Fatso. That nigger won't be bothering you anymore."

Christmas time came and my daddy and brothers went out in the country; cut down a tree. We all decorated it. I was still thinking about that black boy. I was lying on the floor looking up at the blinking lights. "Hey Mama? Do the police have Christmas parties for the people in jail?"

"Well!" she walked toward the kitchen as though she had just remembered something that needed to be taken out of the oven. Then, over her shoulder, "That's a strange question, Elaine. And you're a strange girl."

I was strange and I was too friendly. I understood that. But I wanted to get a new pair of shoes for that black boy, so he wouldn't have to wear torn shoes. I wanted to wrap them up in pretty paper. Maybe his mother wouldn't hate me so, for what I'd done, causing so much trouble, if I got her boy something new and nice for Christmas.

Nobody was talking to me about that boy or what had happened. My mama didn't look at me anymore. She looked over my head and around me. It was clear I had brought shame on my family. Looking at my mama and daddy, I got to thinking they wanted to give me away. I figured they hoped to find another family to claim me, people out in the country who wouldn't be ashamed to have a strange and too-friendly trouble-making girl like me.

One day in January my daddy came to my bedroom door. "Get dressed."

"Where are we going?"

"To the courthouse."

I got dressed. My mother brushed my hair. She didn't look sad, even though this was probably the last time she would ever brush my hair. I hoped the family who got me would be nice about brushing the tangles out of my hair.

I got in Daddy's Studebaker, and we rode down the street, to the courthouse. We got out the car. My daddy held my hand. A policeman met us in the hallway and directed us to a little room. There was a red couch in it. I sat down. My daddy walked back and forth, back and forth.

"What are we doing here?" I dared to ask.

"They want you to identify that colored boy, the one who scared you."

I climbed my Daddy's leg like a chinaberry tree. "No! No! I'm not going to! I'm not going to!" Pee puddled on the floor by my feet.

Daddy walked out of the room. I watched him, brushing himself off and stomping down the hall. I was scared half to death. Because I knew if that black boy saw me, he would point at me and yell, "That's her! That's the girl! She's the one who told lies on me. All I did was talk to her." Then the police would put me or my daddy in jail for lying and causing big trouble.

My daddy came back in the little room, huge in the doorway. "Let's go." I grabbed his outstretched hand.

We went outside and got in the car. Daddy gripped the steering wheel and looked straight ahead. His jaw was working back and forth. "Elaine, don't you ever think about this again. You hear me?" And he bellowed, "I mean it! Don't you even remember any of this!"

I washed my underpants in the bathroom sink when we got home. And I did as I was told. I did not remember a thing about that black boy, the tin roof shanties, or the courthouse. I never looked across that field again. I put the whole thing away where it could never be found. Until now.

Dr. Blankenship listened carefully. He leaned toward me. "So, what are you going to do with this now, now that you know what happened?"

"But I don't know. I still don't know what happened to that boy." Curiosity motivated me to take a road trip, the first road trip I had driven by myself. I took time off from work and drove from our home in Jackson, Tennessee to Gainesville, Florida where I walked through the old neighborhood, visited the public library, and read old local newspapers on microfilm, hoping to find some mention of the incident with the black boy across the field. Carl Reagan was already dead, but I visited others who had been members of the church when I was a child, and I asked them if they remembered what had happened.

I stayed with the Anderson family during my visit. They were excited to see me and happy to host my visit until I asked about Carl Reagan, my daddy and my brother beating up a black boy when I was four years old. Mrs. Anderson got up from the table and began washing dishes. Mr. Anderson ran his hands through his hair and turned away from me. He took a sip from his coffee cup. Then he said, "No. That doesn't even sound right. Your daddy was a good man, a kind man. That's what I remember."

# CHAPTER III

## REDISCOVERY AND BETRAYAL

M arch of 1983, I went to work on an alcohol and drug treatment program, the Rediscovery Unit. They needed an RN on the over-night shift. The pay was good with the shift differential. I could work while my daughter slept, and I could sleep while she went to first grade.

The patients at that time were mostly men who had lost their jobs, or were on the edge of losing their job, due to their heavy drinking and most of them were looking at losing their marriages and their homes. I was amazed by the transformation I witnessed in so many of our patients. They came through our doors looking like a mess, weepy or belligerent, red faced and loud, as we gave them a shot of Valium to calm them and help get through detox. I watched them walk into their first group therapy session with ready resistance.

But groups of recovering people have power. I watched grown men break down and cry about their needs that were not being met, needs that had never been met. And I cried with them. At that time, in the early 80's, insurance allowed patients to stay in treatment for thirty to sixty days. By the time patients walked out of our unit they had often regained their jobs and their marriages. The power of group therapy and 12-Step meetings changed their lives.

Sometimes patients were unable to sleep, and I sat in the community room with them, drank cups of strong coffee and listened to their stories. I shared my story with them. And in doing so I recognized my own needs. I wanted to be honest about my own drinking and drugging. I was drinking beer every day and taking Valium. I didn't have a prescription, but I had a friend, a psychiatrist, who provided me with samples. Getting to know the patients on the unit awakened a hunger in me to be sober, to depend on a power greater than myself rather than to depend on alcohol and Valium to get through the day. I started attending Alcoholics Anonymous meetings where I could express my desire for the gifts of honesty and sobriety. Belonging to a group of recovering people strengthened me personally and professionally. Sobriety made me a better nurse, a better mother, and a better friend to myself. I could see how I had allowed the abusive marriage to damage my self-image. I thought I deserved the abuse, the lies and the cruelty. With a sober mind I began to pay attention to my life in ways that I had not previously. But even sobriety couldn't remove my fear of getting fat. I had deeper healing that needed to be addressed.

A nurse on our unit, Annette Hutchison, was confident in her nursing skill. She had been a missionary in Nigeria, taking care of starving, sick babies under a tent. I admired Annette. She loved Jesus and I wanted to love him too. I wanted something more for my spiritual life than the pious, self-righteousness I had known as a child. I was open to learning. I could feel that my life was on the verge of becoming something new. Annette and I prayed together. I asked God to help me learn to love myself. I wondered if God had the power to heal my bulimia, even as I clung to my determination never to gain weight.

Going to church on Sunday, a United Methodist church, became part of my new life. I took Jennifer and paid attention to what she was learning in Sunday school. The Methodists didn't seem as rigid in their beliefs as the Nazarenes had been and I grew comfortable enough to join the church.

My husband, Doug, and I belonged to the Jackson Writers' Group. It was a group of writers who got together the first Sunday afternoon of every month to share what we had written and to receive encouragement. The refreshments were always wonderful. We all felt the group's gentle pressure to have something new to share each month, a fresh poem, a short story, an essay, or a memoir piece. Each year the group applied for a grant from the Tennessee Arts Commission, asking for funds to publish *The Old Hickory Review*, a poetry journal. Poems were submitted by people from all over the world for our annual publication. In 1983, I was the group's treasurer and Doug was the president. We had just received our funding for the publication, and we had begun the work of selecting poems.

I came home from the Rediscovery Unit one morning and Doug suggested that the two of us take a road trip. "Let's leave Jennifer with Mom and you and I just drive south, see where we end up." And so we did. We drove as far as Oxford, Mississippi where we visited William Faulkner's home, Rowan Oak, and shopped in a downtown bookstore. Then we got a room for the night.

"There's something I need to tell you," Doug said as he stretched out on the bed. "I don't want you to freak out."

I tensed. We had been married for ten years and any time Doug had something important to tell me it had been about a gambling debt. His gambling had started out so benign. He had begun playing pinball and, instead of playing off the games he won, he would have the bartender pay him off in quarters. That led to his betting on games and races. Red, a bookie in town, took his bets and there had been a time when Doug came to me crying. He told me that Red's guys were going to break his legs if he didn't pay up a two-thousand-dollar loss on a football game. I took out a bank loan so Doug's legs could stay unbroken. Now he was stretched out on a bed in a hotel room in Oxford, Mississippi. I waited to hear how much money he needed.

"You know the money we got for the writer's group?"

"The grant money?"

"It's all gone."

"What?"

"I spent it. I'm sorry. Don't freak out. But you shouldn't have left the check book where I could find it."

"I hid it in the closet behind my shoes."

"And that wasn't smart enough because any fool could have found it there."

"What are you saying? The money is gone?" I was having difficulty believing this disaster. "What will we tell the other people in our group?"

Doug sat up straight. "I know what I'll tell them. I'll just remind them who the treasurer is. That's my plan. So, you'd do well to replace the money before any of them find out about it."

"Take me home. Now. I want to go home. I'm not enjoying this road trip at all."

I took out a loan and replaced the money. As far as I know no one in our writing group was ever the wiser for what had happened. The incident clarified my need to get out of the marriage. I began to put money back in a savings account that I kept secret, preparing for an escape. And I embraced daily times of prayer with Annette. I prayed about my attraction to women and how I had made a terrible mistake in thinking that marrying a man would solve that issue. Annette urged caution in my plans to leave the marriage. "You could lose Jennifer if Doug tells the court about your feelings for other women." Doug's rage was not to be taken lightly. Although he had never hit me, he knew how to strike terror and guilty nerves inside my soul.

# Unpardonable Sin

Having Annette as a friend was a stabilizing force in my life. During our time of shared prayer, I confessed about the short-lived affair I had had with my supervisor, Sandra Evans, at the previous hospital where I had worked. The romance began while we were making last rounds on all my patients. Sandra sometimes came to our floor and walked room to room with me, chatting as we checked to make sure all was well with the patients. Most of them were sleeping at 10:45, when I got off my evening shift, so we didn't turn on any lights. We quietly checked to make sure IV fluids were dripping properly, seeing that no one was in pain and that family members had the blankets and pillows they needed. One night, my arm brushed up against Sandra's breast as we leaned over an elderly patient. There was something in the way she reacted that let me know she was not opposed to being touched by me. To be clear, Sandra had also begun taking her evening breaks with me, bringing her dinner to my floor, and offering me bites of whatever she had brought to eat. So that night, the night I first touched her breast, I took a chance when the two of us were alone on the elevator. I reached for her arm, pulled her close and kissed her on the lips. It was quick and it was well received. From that moment on, Sandra and I were looking for opportunities to be alone.

Jennifer was three years old at the time and I took her with me to visit Sandra and her extended family out in Milan, a small town outside Jackson. Sandra's parents fell in love with Jennifer and me. They knew me as a co-worker with their daughter. Staunch Church of Christ people, they believed homosexuality was an unpardonable sin and because of that Sandra felt strongly about keeping our romance a secret. Her family meant the world to her. A single young woman with a nursing degree and a supervisory position, she had made her parents proud. She was active in her church, and she didn't want to jeopardize her good standing among the local Church of Christ folks.

We planned a weekend together. I told Doug I was having a romantic affair with Sandra and that we were going to take a trip. I saw no reason to lie to Doug. Since I had fussed at him for years about his inability to tell the truth, I just told him the truth, that Sandra had something to offer me that he did not have. Sandra told her parents that she was going to Paris Landing and her friend, the other nurse, wanted to have a little vacation with her.

We drove to Paris Landing State Park and got a room at the lodge on the bank of Kentucky Lake. It was a nice room, we agreed, before we tore our clothes off and lunged, as a clinging unit, toward the bed. Hungrily we pawed at one another until we found a rhythm. Our mouths were as busy as our hands, touching and licking at the same time, tasting how good it was to be alone, to feel safe and to satisfy the burning desire to love another woman. The lovemaking did not disappoint either of us. We made love for so long; we almost missed the evening meal at the lodge's restaurant. Sandra stared at me across the table, boldly adoring me. We were among strangers, and she was feeling brave. She reached for my hand under the table and gave it a squeeze. I was enjoying myself.

The next morning Sandra wanted to cross the bridge and go to Shiloh National Forest and the civil war exhibit for the Battle of Shiloh. We ate breakfast downstairs and Sandra walked over to the jukebox. She put four quarters in. I heard them fall. Then she chose songs, the first of which was "Can I Have This Dance?" by Anne Murray. I watched her hips swaying to the music as she selected more tunes. "Would you be my partner and hold me tight? When we're together it feels so right. Can I have this dance for the rest of my life?" I had never felt more loved.

And that might explain what happened next. We got in Sandra's car and rode to the Shiloh Military Park. We watched a film about the history of the Battle of Shiloh. Then we got back in the car and began slowly driving along, getting out to pay homage to war shrines along the way. At a certain statue,

Sandra stopped the car and we both got out of the car. Instead of admiring the civil war soldier, I took off running. I had no idea I was going to do it. I was suddenly and inexplicably possessed by something powerful that threw me into a headlong run. I ran down the hill behind that military monument, through shrubs and undergrowth, then up a hill, scrambling and clawing at the earth to get a leg up. I ran headfirst with no idea where I was going. I was just running because I had to get away. I ran, panting, up another hill, discovering a paved road there, I slowed to a walk. Sandra came around a bend, her car screeching to a halt as I gasped for breath. "Get in!" she bellowed.

I was bleeding in several places where blackberry vines had scratched my arms and legs. Sandra gave the scratches a side long gaze. "What in the world is wrong with you?" She looked at me and then back at the road as she was pulling into traffic. "I mean, you never told me that you have severe psychiatric troubles. Want to fill me in on that now? Because we've got time. I'm driving your ass home and dropping you off there, safe and sound. I'm through with you." Sheepish and ashamed, I stared out the window, not saying a word all the way home.

The next Monday night at work, Sandra came to my floor when it was my usual time for break. She walked into the break room where I was eating a bologna and cheese sandwich. She checked out the space and observed that I was eating alone. She came in, closed the door behind her and sat down in front of me. "Can I have a bite of your sandwich?" she asked. I offered her the sandwich, a sandwich that was missing only one bite, a sandwich I had made at home with great care earlier. Sandra took the sandwich and slowly ate it all, one very deliberate bite at a time. And I sat silently, knowing I deserved her anger. I just couldn't find the courage I needed to say, "I'm sorry but I am scared to death about being a lesbian. It would mean stepping out somewhere beyond where I've been before." Staying in an abusive relationship with a man seemed so much safer to me than living with the woman I adored and who adored me in return. And yet, I was saving money for my getaway.

I told Annette all about Sandra and my regrets about how that had turned out. I had left the hospital where Sandra and I worked together. It was too hard, seeing each other at work. And it was easy for me to get another job. Every clinic and hospital was in need of registered nurses.

Early one morning Sandra came by the Rediscovery unit, and I was surprised to see her. "Are you wanting to stop drinking?" I laughed. Sandra was not one to overindulge in anything, least of all alcohol or drugs.

"No. Just wanting to check on you. Are you happy with Doug? Are you safe and happy there?"

I took a deep breath. I could feel the pull toward Sandra as she stood by the nurses' station. I had not forgotten Paris Landing. But I chose the easier way, nodding emphatically, "Yes, I'm very happy with Doug." It was 1979 and I knew that the courts would award custody of Jennifer to Doug if I left him for love of a woman. Sandra turned and walked away.

A few weeks later Doug came home from his job as the program director at the community mental health center. "Have you heard? That nurse, you know the one you went with to Paris Landing, Sandra? Right. She committed suicide. She was found dead in a hotel room. Yeah. That's right. I'd say she didn't try very hard to live life before she ended it," he smirked. I froze. I was trying so hard to be a good heterosexual wife. I was cooking dinner every evening, praying, going to church on Sunday and spending quality time with our daughter. I wanted to feel nothing about Sandra's death, so I didn't feel a thing. I blocked any emotion and squelched any memory of Sandra. I learned this useful trick when Mr. and Mrs. Spence took me to the motel room. I learned how to do it by watching my mother as she hid behind the chest of drawers with her hands over her eyes as my father beat my naked body. I learned then that I can move things in my mind, distance from reality, move reactions and feelings into dark places with a heavy padlock on them.

"Have you felt anything about it now, now that you've told me about Sandra?" Annette knew how to get right at what was happening with me emotionally. I started crying. In the safety of a friend's apartment, I was able to mourn the loss of Sandra. In the midst of that freeing sob, I considered other losses like the death of my father, and the death of my innocence. I cried a lot that day with Annette as a witness.

# A MIRACLE AND WANTING OUT

O n Thanksgiving Day of 1983, I asked Jennifer and Doug to sit with me and start the day by reading the hundredth Psalm. *Make a joyful noise unto the Lord, all ye lands. Serve the Lord with gladness. Come before his presence with singing*...After that I said a prayer of thanksgiving for our lives and for all the goodness we enjoyed. Then we headed out to Aunt Patty's house for the usual Thanksgiving feast with all of Doug's extended family.

Aunt Patty had insisted on making all the dishes that year. "Just bring yourselves," she said. And we entered the house to find a feast prepared for us. Turkey, ham, corn casserole, broccoli casserole, lima beans, cranberry relish, dressing, mashed potatoes and gravy, sweet potatoes, hot rolls, pickles, pecan pie, pumpkin pie, and carrot cake. We all gathered around the table, a large group of small children, young adults and older folks, aunts, uncles and cousins. Tall candles burned in the center of the table. I was surprised and honored when Aunt Patty called on me to say the blessing. "Lord of life, thank you for this feast. For the opportunity to be together as family. Thank you for the kind hands that prepared this food, and may we receive it with deep gratitude for all the ways you feed us on our journey together. Amen."

We began filling our plates. I got a little of everything and sat down next to Doug and across from Aunt Mary June. We ate our fill. When my plate was emptied, I pushed back from the table with the intention to vomit. It was nothing new or unusual. I had been vomiting most meals for twelve years. Food frightened me; a full stomach terrified me.

But something strange happened as I pushed back from the table to go purge. I was suddenly immersed in what felt like warm oil. I seemed to be standing in a bright place. It was altogether peaceful, more peaceful than any place I had ever been. In that space I didn't hear a voice, but I understood a message. "Elaine, your food is love, one way love is expressed to you. When you eat your food, know that you are loved." It was as simple and strange as that. And then I was back at the table beside Doug and across from Aunt Mary June. It was clear they had not noticed anything out of the ordinary. I took a deep breath as they discussed whether to have cake or pie. Finally, they concluded that having both cake and pie would be their best choice. We laughed and the sound of my laughter shocked me. It came from a full place in my chest. The sound of my laughter was deeper, richer, as though something inside my chest had been set free. I didn't get up and I didn't vomit that meal. But more important, I didn't sweat and tremble with panic as the food digested and warmed my body. Instead of fear, I felt nurtured.

Aunt Patty gave us leftovers to carry home. As the sun set and we drove home, I was awe struck by the beauty of the world around us, the pink and yellow cast across lawns, and the mystery of what had happened to me at the table. It was a miracle. I was sure of that. I was also sure that the miracle would not hold. I assumed I would return to being frightened by food. But that night we heated up the leftovers and ate a meal together while watching the movie, "Camelot." Again, my food felt like a gift of love, and I was amazed by the change that had come over me.

I told Annette about the miracle, and she invited me to tell the story to her Sunday school class. I began telling the story, how I had experienced a miracle, at churches and in recovery groups. Food, the bites that I took, became holy for me and I no longer had to deal with daily shame that had accompanied my vomiting. Always searching for a private bathroom, locking the door, and leaning over a toilet to purge became only a memory as food became my friend rather than my enemy. My weight increased to a hundred and fifteen pounds. But I felt gratitude for the strength I gained, rather than fear of being fat. I took long walks every day, feeling the Spirit of God walking with me and increasing my joy. I told the miracle story at work and invitations started coming for me to share my healing story with church groups, nursing groups and women's gatherings. I wrote the story and submitted it to a Christian magazine, *Christianity Today*. The program directors for Pat Robertson's program, the *700 Club*, read my story, and called, inviting me to Virginia Beach to tell my story on national television.

I began to see myself as a person with a light, a ray of hope for people struggling with food addictions and eating disorders. I came to recognize that I had a gift for storytelling. People enjoyed the sound of my voice and the stories I told. I enjoyed being a whole new person.

One night Doug got out of bed and found me in the dining room, writing in my journal. "What are you doing?" he asked "I'm sick of seeing you always writing in that journal and praying. You call yourself a Christian, but I know who you really are." And he slapped my journal off the table. The healthier I became; the more threatened Doug was becoming. My new self-confidence frightened him, and I could see it. But I didn't know how to help him, and I wasn't willing to give up on my own recovery. I sat and waited for him to take his anger back to bed. Then I picked up my journal and finished writing.

The following night Doug had his own experience with transformation. He says that he was watching television, and a preacher came on the screen, talking about the love of God and the power of God's forgiveness. Doug claims that he heard a call from God as he sat there on the couch in front of the television. He understood God to be calling him to preach. He got up the following day and went to the pastor, Richard Smith, at his family's church, Aldersgate United Methodist, and told Richard that he was going to attend seminary and would be available to serve a Methodist church when and if the door opened. Richard made a few phone calls and within a few weeks Doug was appointed to serve the Pinson Charge, just south of Jackson. It was a head spinning transformation and I believed, with a bit of skepticism, that Doug was truly transformed. Mostly, I hoped his gambling days were over.

While everything seemed to change in our lives, some things stayed the same. We moved into a house in south Jackson, closer to the two churches Doug was called to serve. Jennifer started attending a new school. She was in the fourth grade. I kept my job at the Rediscovery Unit while Doug preached, provided pastoral care, and drove to Memphis for classes at Memphis Theological Seminary. Some nights he stayed there when it was more convenient for him than driving home.

One afternoon I was cooking dinner and Doug was in the back bathroom. We were chatting from one room to the other and I got tired of yelling through the house, so I walked to the bathroom door and continued talking. Doug quickly slammed the door in my face. I had just caught a glimpse of him washing his shirt in the bathroom sink. That was not a usual thing. I had never seen him hand wash anything he owned. "Stay out of the bathroom when I'm in here," he demanded. I shrugged. Sometimes he was the strangest person. I went back to cooking dinner.

That same week I read in the newspaper about brown recluse spiders. I learned that they like dusty, hot, unused spaces like the attic or closet floors. That motivated me to open all our closet doors. I pulled everything out and vacuumed each one. When I pulled the shoes and belts out of Doug's closet, I found one of his white shirts balled up on the floor. I picked it up to hang it when I noticed the shirt was damp and there was something red on the collar. Lipstick. Unmistakable lipstick. And it was smudged. I could tell instantly that this was the shirt Doug had been hand washing.

Part of me took delight in this find. I stood there and smiled to myself. If Doug was getting lipstick on his collar over at the seminary, I didn't have to feel so badly about falling in love with this woman and that woman. At that very moment, I was still stunned by Sandra's death. I was doing my best as a preacher's wife. But all the same, if Doug had a girlfriend, this might be my ticket out of the marriage. I looked forward to Doug's return home that day.

He came home and we hugged and kissed. I made dinner and Jennifer told us about her day at school. When she went upstairs with a neighbor friend, I tapped Doug on the shoulder as he sat staring at his computer screen. "I found this shirt in your closet today."

"What the hell! What are doing snooping in my closet?"

"I was cleaning. I cleaned out all the closets today, including yours. I had no idea that your closet was off limits to me since I am the one who washes your clothes and puts them away in that closet every week."

"Well, I'm telling you now. Stay out of my closet." He turned away as though our conversation was finished.

"You want to talk to me about the lipstick on your collar?"

"It was a joke."

"A joke?"

"Yes, a joke. Some of the guys at the seminary were horsing around and they smeared lipstick on my collar. Stupid prank."

"Oh. Is that why you were being all sneaky the other day, washing the shirt in the back sink, then trying to hide it on the floor of your closet? Why not just drop the shirt in the laundry like you always do?"

"Because you are such a snoopy bitch. That's why. I didn't put my shirt in the laundry because I knew what you would think."

"And what would I think?"

"I know you and your suspicious ideas. If you want to know the truth, that lipstick belonged to a woman in Memphis. I have been helping her. She's a stripper at Platinum Plus and she has three kids. I've been helping her with some of her bills and she wanted to kiss me for my help. So there. I'll have you know that you are the only one in this relationship who has been unfaithful. So go suck on that, why don't you?"

What he said was true and it stung. Reminding me of my own sinfulness with Sandra backed me away from Doug and I dropped the subject of lipstick. I just kept it like a secret weapon in the dark dusty corner of my mind. I didn't want Doug to start listing the multiple times I had been unfaithful to our marriage. I couldn't let go of Sally Moretti. I loved her and I never quit missing her. Being married, I realized, was not a cure. I desired something more than what I was getting from Doug. I wanted to be noticed and valued. I was tired of being used and I was tired of using Doug.

I needed a way out of the marriage. When I caught Doug in a soft place, when he seemed open to rational discussion, when Jennifer was out playing with her friends I might say openly, "I need to get out of this marriage, Doug. This isn't working for either one of us. I'm not mad. I just need a chance to be who I am." I apologized repeatedly for starting our relationship and for any pain I had caused. I just wanted out.

"Go ahead," he would say. "The door is open. Always is. But believe me when I say you'll never get to see Jennifer. I'll tell the judge that you're a lesbian and I'll be granted full custody. Go on. Leave." What he said was true. I would shrug and head off to do the laundry or vacuum the den. While I couldn't control Doug or my situation right away, I could keep a clean house while I waited for better days.

# WHAT WOULD JESUS DO?

O ne day I got a phone call from a member of Doug's church. I was working nights and sleeping during the day, so I did my best to sound alert when I heard the anguish in Rita English's voice. "My son just died all alone in a hospital in Memphis."

"Oh Rita. Oh, Rita."

"He had AIDS. I didn't even know he was sick. He never told me."

"Oh."

"And they're saying he had a partner. They're telling me that our Keith was gay."

I was sitting up in bed by then. And trying to think of something comforting or helpful to say. But again, all I could think to say was, "Oh, Rita. I am so sorry."

The loss of her oldest child was an enormous tragedy compounded by the funeral home's refusal to pick up Keith's body at the morgue. "We can't afford to contaminate one of our vehicles." She kept calling until she found a funeral home that would lay her son to rest. But we were all unprepared for our church family's resistance to having Keith's body and his funeral at the church. "We don't need that kind of thing in our sanctuary," Ernest Blanks explained to a distraught and grieving mother. I went to the English's home and sat with Rita and her husband, Darin. We drank coffee, more than a pot of coffee, around the table. I couldn't think of any other way to feel helpful. Somebody once told me, "If you don't know what's right to do in a case with death, go toward the pain. Don't run from it."

Doug met with the church board and talked with his district superintendent. I gave a nurse's report to the board, educating them regarding the AIDS virus. "Having Keith's body in the sanctuary will not jeopardize the health of anyone in attendance at the funeral," I assured them. But there was more. It wasn't just the fear of infection that was fueling the men's resistance. They were disgusted to learn that one of their own, a boy they had watched grow up, a young man who had played piano and sang so many Gospel tunes during worship, was homosexual. They could hardly speak the word. It came out with bitterness and anger.

"I think," Doug rang a small bell and got the attention of his church leaders. "I think we should consider what Jesus would have done if he were here tonight. I can't imagine he would have told a grieving mother and father, sisters and brother, that their family could not have a service in the family's place of worship. I can't imagine that at all. Not the Jesus I know. Not the defender of orphans, widows, the poor and the outcast. Don't forget how he touched the leper and healed him when nobody else would get anywhere close to him. I say we have the funeral here and that we grieve with Rita and Darin."

The little clapboard church on a country corner was full on Monday afternoon. About twelve of us had to sit up front in the choir loft to make room for all the family and friends. Keith had been well loved. He was a talented kid, a good student and cute as could be. He had moved to Memphis only a few years before his death and, although he called regularly, he stopped coming home to visit. Now the community gathered to mourn his loss. Rita English came through the doors of that church, after everyone was seated, with her arms upraised and her face lifted to the ceiling. She opened her mouth and began singing the Doxology, *Praise God from whom all blessings flow! Praise him all creatures here below. Praise him above you heavenly hosts. Praise Father, Son and Holy Ghost.* She walked to the closed casket and put her head on the spread of roses.

Doug and I would not learn until the following day that some of the men had stationed themselves in the church parking lot, armed, and *ready to shoot any goddamned Memphis queer that tries to attend this service.*

135

# My Writing Days

The bishop and his cabinet moved Doug from serving in Tennessee. They moved him to Kentucky. Doug's income increased. We moved into the parsonage, and we planned on my not taking a job. I could write instead of working as a nurse. This was another miracle. We turned the third bedroom into my writing room. It was my job. I went to my writing room every day and wrote for hours. I had pieces published in The Upper Room, Sunday school papers, Christian magazines, and poetry journals. I wrote the entire manuscript for a book of family devotions. I sent that out to four publishers. But all four rejected it, an unsolicited manuscript. My writing was my therapy in our Kentucky home. I resented no one or nothing so long as I had time and a place to write.

During my writing days, I was being called on to share my story of healing at various Methodist churches in the area. I was receiving invitations to preach on Sunday mornings. Church leaders were inviting me to fill in on Sunday mornings when the regular pastor was sick or if he and his family had gone away on vacation. I began to write sermons. And I looked at the idea of going to seminary. I would have to earn a bachelor's degree if I wanted to be accepted into graduate school. I looked over at the University of Tennessee at

Martin, just a few miles away from our home. And I applied for grants and gifts while I enrolled in the university, declaring a major in English. Methodist churches are very generous with people who feel called to serve God in their denomination. Along with the assistance I received from the Methodists, I had to work part time as a nurse to afford my return to college. But it was well worth it. I worked part time on the psych ward at the hospital in Union City.

I was introduced to the study of philosophy by Dr. Louis Malden, who so engaged me in his class discussions that I changed my major to a double major: English and philosophy. Dr. Malden made us think and he wanted us to struggle with ideas. The eighteen- and nineteen-year-olds in the class were yawning. But I, a thirty-nine-year-old who had been out in the work world for two decades, was enthralled by the chance to ask some bigger questions. Who are we? Why are we here? How should we live our lives?

I took a course in the biology building, Ecology. Oh! that class! It blew my mind completely. I would say it was the most sacred class I ever attended. The burly professor was a no-frills kind of guy. Nothing warm or fuzzy about him. But the content of what he taught was like poetry. "Everything is connected," I heard him saying. "Everything touches." I liked that and I liked learning about rainwater running downhill, picking up nutrients that would feed the pond at the bottom of the hill and the fish in the pond as well as turtles. Cows drink from the pond and humans drink the cow's milk. The birds get in on this too; everything in nature's system has a give and take. I loved learning.

All of this learning and thinking and writing papers somehow got the attention of the bishop and his cabinet. They heard about my filling in the pulpits around the conference and "Would I be interested in serving a charge of my own?" I was appointed by the bishop and the cabinet to serve The Union City Circuit, a charge that included four small congregations: Rives, Antioch, Beech Bluff and Mount Manuel. Sharon Oglesby would be my district superintendent.

Methodist ministers know each other. They have weekly cluster gatherings; monthly district meetings and entire conferences meet annually. Everybody knows one another and sizes up one another in terms of who has won the bishop's eye? Who among us will get the big church? Who will be the next bishop? It's a competitive thing because not everybody can serve a big church with a hefty salary. Most Methodist churches are small and out in rural areas, located on the same property as a cemetery. There might be no more than ten people in regular attendance, but the church was good enough for grandpa; it's too good to let go. Methodist preachers get together to make friends and to create alliances. It's mostly a guy thing. But Sharon Oglesby came into the picture and shook things up at the Memphis Annual Conference. She was the first woman to serve on the bishop's cabinet in the Memphis area. Many were heard to complain and grouse, jealous twitter around Memphis and its Methodists. Things were changing and that meant a woman would be a district superintendent, a woman would preside over a man's own charge conference, the local church's annual business meeting. This required much adjustment of jock straps and suspenders.

Born and raised in Memphis, Sharon had been the apple of her parents' eye. They adored her and her brothers. They raised their daughter to believe she could meet whatever goal she set for herself. So, when the Spirit called her to preach, her parents, who wondered if a woman should or could lead a church, had to bite their tongues, and encourage their youngest child to follow her call.

She did well in the system. Sharon was pretty and petite, the kind of woman who shops at Talbot's. She dressed smartly. Sharon was shaped nicely and had a perkiness in her step that made her alluring. With dark hair framing her valentine shaped face, she was undeniably beautiful. Her blue eyes were lively and let you know she was expecting to win at whatever the challenges. She married well. Her perseverance, over time in a male-dominated system, caught the bishop's eye. And thus, she was invited to serve on his cabinet.

I learned that Sharon had much to do with my being called to serve the Union City Circuit. "The guys were all saying that they had no place that would accept a woman preacher. So, I said, *Send her to me*." She placed me in her district, announcing to the Union City charge conference, "You are getting the best preacher you ever had, and you will undoubtedly mourn on the day she leaves you." I suppose she got complaints, but she never told me about them. She just welcomed me to her district and gave me her phone number. "Call me if you need me," she said.

I had Sharon to thank for noticing my gifts and for fighting for me to have a place where I could contribute those gifts. I loved serving those four Methodist churches in Union City. Each place had a distinct personality, and I recognized their differences, nevertheless I wanted all four of the churches to do something together. It would be a first, each church council warned me. But I hoped it would not be the last time the four churches enjoyed each other's company. I planned a play, an Easter play titled, *The Women of Easter*. The cast and crew would require participation from all four churches. There would be lighting, filming, sound, singing, acting, keyboard playing, set design and construction, and costume design. Everybody needed to chip in where their gifts took them. Some people just gave money for the scripts and costumes. And that was acceptable. Although the men who drove out to the highway and picked up the huge stone that I wanted on stage deserve as much or more credit than anyone else. That stone still sits outside the front doors of the church. No one has forgotten our Easter play. All four churches had a good time making it happen together.

I graduated from UT Martin *magna cum laude* while I served those four little churches. And then it was time for me to attend the same seminary that Doug had attended, Memphis Theological Seminary. Doug made it clear that he preferred my being the preacher's wife rather than being another preacher.

"Clergy couples have a hard time getting good appointments," he complained. "But there's no use talking to you when you've got your mind made up."

My mind was made up and I had Sharon to thank, again, when I was appointed to serve a three-church circuit, the Gates Circuit, made of Gates, Concord and Eureka United Methodist Churches. Gates was closer to Memphis, making the drive more convenient for my seminary classes. Doug was furious about my appointment, blaming Sharon because my appointment seemed to him a better appointment than the appointment he got. "Damn that Sharon and her loyalty to you! I'd like to pinch her pretty little head off," he groused as he helped me unload my things at the Gates parsonage. It was a three-bedroom brick house next door to the church in Gates. I planned to use the house as my office, and I would hold committee meetings there.

As we were carrying boxes of books into the house, Linda Dickson, the church's treasurer, pulled up in the driveway. "Hi there! You must be our new little preacher."

"Hello. Yes. I'm Elaine."

"Can I call you Elaine or should I say Pastor Elaine?"

"Just Elaine is fine."

"Great. Well, I came by to give you your paycheck. No point in making you wait until Sunday to get it."

"Thanks. I didn't expect that. How nice."

"Well, some of us really hope you have a nice experience here. So don't you pay any attention to those folks who are asking what we did wrong to be given a woman for our preacher." She laughed. "I say a woman can do anything a man can do and do it better because she must. I'm here for you, honey. And I'm not the only one who is willing to give you a fair chance. Keep that in mind." She nodded at Doug and Jennifer and then gave me a hug along with the check. With a cheerful wave, she was off again.

Doug chuckled. "I bet Sharon can't make *all* your troubles go away."

I was no longer on Sharon's district; Ken Burnett was my new boss. But Sharon lived only a few minutes away from the parsonage at Gates. We started meeting every afternoon to walk together. Sharon was accustomed to city life, but her position placed her in a very small town. Her close friends had backed off from her since she got into a position with power in the conference. Her job as a district superintendent was all about putting out fires. Nobody needed her until the trouble was out of control. That's when her phone rang. It was the kind of job that can destroy a person's faith in the goodness of humanity. She needed a friend. Sharon's husband, Rick, was the quiet type. He wasn't happy to be the preacher's husband in a small town; it wasn't the kind of thing he could brag about to other guys. But he was willing to go along if it meant there would be no argument. He read his newspapers and fiddled with antique cars. He knew better than to stand in Sharon's way when God and the bishop called.

I started feeling more than gratitude toward Sharon. We walked together in the afternoons and talked on the phone most evenings. It was good to have another woman to confide in, somebody who understood our situation and knew the personalities involved. Sharon and I let off steam on our walks and in our phone conversations. I could make her laugh and that made me feel so close to Sharon. I began to think of her as my lover, not that we had ever been intimate in any way and not that I thought that would ever be a possibility. Her boundaries were clear. But I fantasized about having her all to myself. I took every opportunity to be with Sharon. I threw a surprise birthday party for her when she turned fifty. I paid attention to her needs and did my best to meet them.

One afternoon Sharon and I were walking on a track, round and round the asphalt, just stretching our legs and talking. I reached out and took her hand. We held hands for a bit before she pulled away. On another occasion, I managed to be Sharon's roommate for a night in a hotel during the annual conference in Paducah. I hardly slept that night, hungrily listening to the sound of Sharon's breathing, in her own bed, but so close to me. It would have been possible for me to get on the edge of my bed, stretch my arm out, reach and touch her. It was that close, and I imagined kissing every inch of her tiny body.

It was during that time, while I was falling in love with Sharon, two women who belonged to my Concord Church stopped by the parsonage. I made coffee and we sat together at the kitchen table. Gail and Tammy were mother and daughter, both farmer's wives. They said they had something to tell me. And they seemed reluctant to spit it out.

With a sheepish grin, Gail confessed, "We go to Tunica pretty often."

"What's that?" I sipped my coffee.

"It's a town in north Mississippi with a bunch of casinos. We go there to have some fun, play the slots."

"Oh. OK."

"We are embarrassed to admit that to you. You might think poorly of us for gambling. We just take a hundred dollars each and we've never lost much. But we're telling you about it because we think you ought to know we see your husband there every time we go. And he's not playing around. He's a serious gambler…"

"There's a whole town dedicated to gambling?" I was trying to picture this in my mind. Right away I knew that this would be like heaven to Doug. He denied gambling, but I knew from our lack of funds that his money was being poured out somewhere. And this information about a place called Tunica explained where my husband was when he gave shady answers for where he'd been over night.

"It's just south of Memphis," Tammy offered.

Jennifer was a senior in high school, a smart and sensitive kid. I was proud of her and the way she had adjusted to the changes in our lives over the past five years. She was aware of her father's gambling troubles. He had stolen her birthday money more than once. The worst and most shameful experience had been when he stole the piggy bank of one of Jennifer's friends. We both knew he had a problem, but because Doug refused to admit that his gambling was a problem, we all lived with the consequences of his addiction and his lies.

Learning about a town full of casinos discouraged me. I had been praying for a miracle, asking God to change Doug, to allow him to ask for help for his gambling addiction. But as Gail and Tammy left the parsonage and I washed our coffee cups, I realized my prayer for a miracle needed to broaden. Maybe the change needed to come from me. I had the savings account I had been keeping for just such a time as this. I could leave the marriage finally. It was time. Jennifer was old enough to have a say about who got custody of her in a divorce settlement. I dried the cups and put them away and made up my mind to move into the parsonage at Gates, to make it home for Jennifer and me, rather than simply my office and meeting space.

# CHAPTER IV

## LEAVING THE MARRIAGE

I was seeing a therapist in Memphis, Elaine Horrell. "I think it's time for me to leave the marriage. I can't stay any longer. It feels like I am supporting Doug's gambling problem by acting as if everything in our life is normal and fine. It's not." Elaine promised to be there for me, and she commended my courage. I trusted her. I had been seeing her weekly since I started classes at the seminary.

That afternoon I picked up Jennifer at school and I explained to her that I was going to move into the parsonage at Gates. "I'll fix one of the bedrooms for you so you can stay with me as often as you want." I explained. "I just need to get away from your dad and I hope that my leaving the marriage will be a wake-up call to him." She understood.

I filled the back seat of my Chevrolet with everything I felt I had to have—linens, clothes and personal hygiene things. The dishes, pots and pans, the silverware, all could stay with him. I just wanted out and material things didn't seem all that important to me. Jennifer went with me that first night and we both slept in the Gates parsonage. Doug was away. He said he was visiting members of his church in a Memphis' hospital.

I took Jennifer to school the next morning and then I called the members of my pastor-parish relations committee. "We need to meet," I said. "I have moved into your parsonage to live there, and I have left the marriage. You need to know what's happening and I will need your support."

The seven members of the committee met in the parsonage. Thelma Voss brought blankets and pillows. Linda Dickson brought a set of cookware and knives. Harriet Gaines brought bags of groceries. I was overwhelmed by their kindness. It was Thelma who spoke first when we all got seated. "If you're unhappy in that marriage, then it's high time you got out of it. There's nothing more any of us need to say other than how can we help you?"

But Lois Jennings was not happy. "All of this kindness and support might be nice. But I want to know what you all are planning to do when *nobody* comes to our churches anymore. Huh? Because it's bad enough that we have a woman for a preacher; the Baptists and all the Church of Christ folks are talking about that. Now if we have a *divorced* woman for a preacher we might as well close those doors because—I am telling you—nobody is going to come to our church."

"I'll be there," Thelma said. Linda and Harriet agreed.

Thelma put her hand on my knee, "We'll take it one day at a time. First thing is to make sure you and Jennifer are safe."

The next day I took Jennifer to school and drove into Memphis for my classes. I told my friends and a few of the faculty members that I had left the marriage. I would need their support.

When Jennifer and I returned to our house in Gates we found shattered glass on the kitchen floor. Someone had broken into the house. We were in no doubt about who had done the damage. We looked around and could find nothing missing. We had left no money or checkbooks in the house, so Doug didn't steal money. We were mystified as to why he had broken into the house. "Just being mean," Jennifer concluded.

But Doug called that night, and he explained why he had broken into our place. "I've got your journals. I've got written proof that you are a lesbian. And I plan to take these journals to Ken Burnett. You're finished in the Methodist Church. Just wait 'til the other clergy people find out about all the love poems you've written to Sharon Oglesby. She's about to get her come-uppance too."

Ken Burnett was my district superintendent. If he found out about my attraction to women, he could remove me from my appointment. The United Methodist Book of Discipline stated plainly: *We do not ordain self-avowed, practicing homosexuals.* Although I had not yet been ordained in the Methodist Church, I was in the formal process to ordination. I had found the courage to move into the parsonage at Gates. That was a first step. I had secured support from Jennifer, my therapist, and my friends. But none of them could help me now that Doug was intent on outing me as a lesbian.

I started to cry. It wasn't just a few tears. My whole body got involved in the sobbing. I sat down at my desk and sobbed. I needed help. More help than I knew how to get. I called Elaine and through my tears I explained that I was at the end of my rope.

"Let me help you, Elaine," she offered. "I'm going to make a phone call and set up an appointment for you with a psychiatrist, Dr. Nancy Duckworth. Is that ok with you?"

I made it through that night, sweeping up the glass on the kitchen floor and calling the chairperson of the properties committee to find someone to repair the kitchen door.

I took Jennifer to school and then I drove to Memphis where I met with the psychiatrist. Dr. Duckworth asked very few questions. I had begun to sob as soon as I sat down in her office. It seemed like all the tears I had held back for years were now pouring out. "I'm going to admit you to Methodist Hospital, give you a break from taking care of other people. Let's let some nurses take care of you for a change. How about that?"

I was more than willing to be cared for. And I had no resistance to being helped. I was open to the men coming, faceless men wearing their white coats. It had come that far with me. I drove to the hospital and was admitted. I called Doug and asked him to pick up Jennifer at school. I asked him to tell her where I was and that I would call her after she got home. Then I called my mother. "Mama, I'm in the hospital."

"Are you hurt?" she was alarmed.

"No, not injured. I'm in the hospital to get some emotional support."

"Honey, you're not on another psychiatric unit, are you?"

"Yes. I'm admitted for depression."

"But you're not depressed. Honey, you've got a nice life. Now you just need to pull yourself together."

"I've left the marriage, Mama. I can't live with Doug anymore."

"What? Oh honey. Now that's a mistake. You get yourself up and out of that hospital right this instant and you make that marriage work. You've got a fine Christian husband, and you certainly don't want to be a divorcee."

"Mama, this marriage was a mistake from the beginning, and you know that. I need your support."

"Your marriage to Doug may have been a mistake from the beginning, but you made your vows, and you need to keep them."

"I don't think I can talk with you anymore. I need to cry."

That afternoon I called Doug's parsonage and asked to speak to Jennifer. "She's busy doing her homework," Doug said. "I told her you don't want her to see you in the hospital."

"But that's not true," I sobbed. Then I called my friend, Gail Gaddie. Gail was in seminary with me and serving churches in Mason, Tennessee. I told her I was in the hospital for depression. "I can't stop crying. Doug has told Jennifer that I don't want to see her and I do want to see her. More than anything." Gail drove to Henning, an hour away from her home, and picked up Jennifer, then she drove to Memphis, bringing Jennifer to see me. The three of us visited and I had a chance to tell Jennifer I would be all right, but I needed some help. Then Gail drove Jennifer back home to Henning. I will never forget Gail's kindness. When I think of the word, friendship, I think of Gail.

I stayed in the hospital for a week. In group therapy, I practiced speaking up for myself. I worked on valuing my feelings. And I started taking medication, Zoloft, for my depression. Dr. Duckworth held individual sessions with me each evening. When it was time for me to be discharged, I was nervous about seeing Doug, worried about my church members' reaction to my having been in a psychiatric unit and scared that Ken Burnett was planning to fire me from my job as pastor to the Gates churches. I had made progress emotionally, but my problems remained to be solved.

I called my therapist and told her I was being discharged. "I plan to stop in Henning and pick up Jennifer if she wants to come with me. But I'm so scared to see Doug." Elaine offered to come with me. She followed me from Memphis to Henning. She walked right into Doug's house and stood like a sentry while I collected a few things and invited Jennifer to come with me. Doug sat on the couch and stared. As I made my last trip across the room, he asked, "Isn't there anything about me that you have loved?"

"Many things. I loved many things about you. But it's time for both of us to move on. There's been enough hurt."

The next day I drove to the district office. While I was afraid to learn what my superintendent had to say about my journals and their content, not knowing was terrifying for me. "Did you read my journals?" I asked as we settled into our chairs in his office.

"No. I certainly did not. Doug brought them to me, and I told him in no uncertain language that I would never read someone's private journals, certainly not without their permission."

"Thank you. Did he tell you why he wanted you to read what I wrote?"

"He said you are attracted to women sexually and I told him he had no business telling me something like that."

"It's true. I am attracted to women. And I will finish the year at Gates Circuit. But after that I need to leave my process toward ordination. I'll return to working as a nurse. Being a pastor isn't working out for me."

"Elaine, I don't need to tell you that your church members are very happy with you. You've grown those churches in the year you've been there. They're excited about the programs you've offered them. I hear good things about your preaching and your weekly Bible studies."

"I need to go."

"You don't have to leave the process toward ordination. You can just keep your feelings for women a secret. Nobody has to know."

"But it's keeping secrets that's making me sick."

# LEAVING THE CHURCH

"**Y**ou are certainly free to do what you need to do to care for yourself. But I want you to know I support you staying with us and, if you insist on leaving us, I'll support you in that decision as well." I have always appreciated Ken for his kindness and integrity. He was doing his best to understand my situation.

As part of my seminary course, *The Mission of the Church,* I did an internship with the Lauderdale County Domestic Violence Prevention Program. I spent Thursday evenings hanging out at the shelter, just getting to know the mothers and children who were sheltered there and playing games, eating dinner. I gave Monday afternoons to answering crisis calls. As the fall leaves began to shine in full oranges, yellows and red, I was feeling really connected to the three women in the shelter. They were grateful to be alive and in a safe space. And they were anxious to find a way to get on with their lives. I baked a casserole in the shelter's kitchen and stirred a pot of green beans on the stove. Simple stuff. But it brought us together and we got to know each other there.

October turned into November and all of us were talking about Thanksgiving. None of the women in the shelter knew what to expect this year. They couldn't be with their families for fear of being beaten to death. But they felt like visitors in the shelter; no way to plan when one is a guest in a house, when a person is a victim of violence. We all talked about special recipes and our favorite holiday dishes. It was fun to talk about food. But none of us knew what Thanksgiving would be like this year. The sheltered women had no plans other than staying hidden.

I had always gone to Aunt Patty's house with Doug and Jennifer. For twenty years that had been my Thanksgiving Day plan. Aunt Patty had cooked that miraculous meal at Thanksgiving, the meal that I first digested as absolute love. But now I was separated from Doug. We were not yet divorced but that was coming. I had already been to see a lawyer in Memphis. And my mother wasn't happy with me for leaving my husband. I wouldn't feel welcome there. I had no holiday plans either.

The week before Thanksgiving I got an inspiration. While eating with the women, I asked, "Why don't all of you come over to my house for Thanksgiving?" The idea was an instant success. Plans were quickly made regarding shopping and making favorite dishes. I got a pad of paper and began scribbling a grocery list. And the plan was made. I would go by the shelter and pick up half the women and their families and my friend, Cindy, who was a member of the Eureka

Church, would pick up the others. When the church women heard about my plan to host the shelter guests, they insisted on helping. On Thanksgiving morning, my kitchen counter was covered with dishes and plates: fruit salad, canned tomatoes, pecan pie, sweet potato casserole, spaghetti with sauce, ham slices and hot rolls. I had baked a turkey and made dressing. The women brought their favorite vegetable dishes and desserts. We had a feast!

There was a man, Coot, in Gates, a middle-aged white man, who had been beaten and traumatized by a gang of roughnecks. Coot lived in an abandoned sharecropper shack out in the cotton field. Everybody knew Coot hung out there. He had no running water or any kind of plumbing. He just walked into town each day and begged from folks who stopped at the café. He bought what he needed for the day from Martha's General Store. Gates was a very small farm town. Everybody knew everybody, especially strange folks like Coot.

I knew Coot had a cat and a litter of kittens in that shack. I had stopped by one day, just being neighborly. And Coot had shown me the mother cat and her nursing kittens. I had started picking up cans of cat food when I grocery shopped, dropping them off for Coot and his little furry family. Coot didn't talk. He just grunted and pointed. It seemed to be a holdover from the beating incident. People in town said Coot's head had taken a terrible beating.

I asked permission, before I invited Coot. I asked the women in the shelter if having a man at our Thanksgiving table would cause them discomfort. I described Coot for them and asked if I could include him in our Thanksgiving plans. No one objected at all.

Coot sat at the table with us on Thanksgiving Day. And when the pie was eaten and coffee served, Coot got up from the table and moved over to an easy chair. He pulled a harmonica out of his pocket and began to play. We had after dinner music with tall candles glowing warmly in the center of our table. Coot entertained us all.

I had been told that the three congregations on my charge did not do things together. There was a rift or bad blood, some fear of others being uppity. I was told they liked staying apart from one another. But as I saw my second Christmas season coming with the churches, I suggested that we do a Christmas pageant that would include everybody's children and grandchildren. I gently suggested that we hold the pageant in the middle church, Concord, but Eureka would oversee building the set and Gates would oversee bringing desserts. Everybody had a part to play. And so, the plan was made. We all agreed to meet on Tuesday nights to rehearse, make costumes and build the set.

One Tuesday night I noticed Kay, the mother of three little children, crying. She was trying to hide her crying behind a handkerchief. But I saw it. When everyone was leaving the church I stopped Kay, "Is something hurting you?"

"Oh, I hate to tell you this, but my sister is running from the law. There's a warrant out for her arrest. And she's in a beat-up old Toyota with the back windshield missing. She's living in that old car."

"That's awful," I offered as Kay secured her three children in her car.

"What's most awful," Kay continued, "is that my sister, Leigh, is on the run with a three-month-old baby girl in that beat up car with her."

"Oh no."

"Yes. And Leigh keeps calling me, asking me to take the baby girl so the state won't take her and put her in foster care."

"Oh, I see."

"Well, there's more to be seen," Kay shook her head, "see that little girl in the backseat?" She pointed to Victoria.

"Yes."

"Well, she's not my daughter. She is my niece. I took her three years ago when my sister went into jail."

"Oh."

"Yeah. It's tough because my husband, Eric, was just laid off. And with Christmas coming, we can't afford to take on a baby. We just can't."

I walked to the car door with Kay and assured her I would be in prayer for her and for her family, including her sister and that baby. "What's the baby's name?" I asked.

"Katy, Katy Grace," Kay answered.

I remembered all of them in my morning prayers, asking God to help Kay's family with all their needs. My prayer life was a stabilizing force for me. Every morning, I sat with God and imagined the day before me, journaling about my hopes and fears, turning the day and my needs over to God, thanking God for my continued sobriety. On Friday of that week, I had no classes to attend at the seminary. I sat with my prayer time longer than usual. I prayed for the members of my congregations, and I prayed for our Christmas pageant. And that's when it hit me. We could give that baby girl a place to be safe and warm. Jennifer and I had a third bedroom that was empty in our parsonage. We could move over and make room for one more person. I got up and called Kay. "When you hear from your sister, tell her she can bring the baby. Jennifer and I will take care of her. I would love to have a baby in the house."

So it was that on December 8, 1993, a baby girl was placed in my arms. And we also got a cardboard box that had baby bottles, cigarettes, a lighter and one unopened can of formula. "Jennifer," I said, "we've got to go to the grocery store." Jennifer was sitting at the kitchen table, holding the baby. "Her name is Katy," I said. "Katy Grace."

We went to the grocery store and bought several cans of formula to match the one can Katy had come with. We bought diapers and pacifiers. We found some t-shirts for infants on a rack by the formula. Then we took the baby back home. Taking the bottles out of the cardboard box, I boiled them, along with the nipples. Jennifer walked into the kitchen as I dropped plastic bottles into boiling water. "Mama?" I thought she was going to ask me something. "I admire you more than anybody I know." That moment means as much or more to me than any moment I have ever lived.

That night I put a pillow in a big wicker basket, covered the pillow with a sheet and put Katy Grace in it to sleep beside me. She slept soundly all night long. Jennifer and I were amazed at what a difference one night of good sleep had made on Katy's face and demeanor. "She's so resilient!" we both said it at the same time.

Katy Grace inspired much generosity from the church women in my three congregations. Word got out that there was a baby in the parsonage and by noon of the first day she spent with us, Katy had a crib, a car seat, a playpen, clothes, booties, dresses, blankets, and toys. Everybody wanted a chance to hold Katy and many pictures were taken. Sharon Oglesby came over and brought a red velvet dress and tiny black shoes. On her second night with us, Katy had her own bed in her own bedroom.

Christmas time got closer, and Katy got a part in the pageant. She was a bright yellow star. Sam, one of the Jenkin's boys, held her up high as the wise men followed with their gifts. She was a star for Jennifer and me as well. Having a baby with us made it easier to accept a holiday that was just us. Katy stayed with us through February when Kay's mother, Katy Grace's grandmother, agreed to take her. Letting go of Katy Grace was one of the hardest things I've ever done. I wasn't convinced her grandmother's house was the best place for her to be. But the court said the child was awarded to the next of kin, the grandmother. We had to let her go.

As a local pastor, moving in the process toward ordination, I had a supervising elder, Gary Moore, another Methodist minister who was assigned to go through a workbook with me. I continued meeting with him. He had no idea, I assumed, of what had happened with my journals and Ken Burnett. I would let him know sometime later that I planned to drop out of the process in June.

Gary and I went through the pages of the workbook as we had done in previous meetings together. I got up and picked up my purse. "I'm heading home to do laundry," I said as I started to leave.

"Just another minute," Gary stopped me. "There's something I feel the need to talk to you about." I stood in the doorway and waited. "Please," he continued, "sit back down." I sat down. "I don't know if you're aware of this. But people all over the Memphis conference are talking about you."

"They are?"

"Yes, and the scuttlebutt says that you, well, that you like women. And Sharon Oglesby in particular. I don't know what's true and what's not true with those bits of gossip, but I think you deserve to know and, as your supervising elder, I feel it is my responsibility to ask you about it. Do you like women? I mean, are you like that?"

"I'll tell you what I'm like, Gary. I'm like the kind of woman who does not go around spreading gossip about other clergy on our conference. That's what I am like. I have enough on my own plate to deal with without causing trouble for anybody else. I think I know where that gossip came from and let's just say that who I like is my business and none of yours or anybody else's." I stood and left Gary's office for the last time.

When I got home, the phone was ringing. It was Sharon Oglesby. "Elaine, I've just heard from the bishop. There's some gossip about you and somehow, I've been thrown into a mess that belongs to you. Let me be very clear here. We are not friends. Don't come over here and don't call me. Our friendship has ended. Got it?"

I thought I was going to suffocate. I hung up the phone and crumbled into my desk chair. My throat refused to open and allow breath in or out. I had a lump in my throat the size of a golf ball that ached so badly I thought my throat would burst. I hugged myself and rocked back and forth, back and forth. I started to moan. I moaned and rocked.

When I started breathing again, I went to the high school to pick up Jennifer and I told her that Doug had spread rumors about me among the other clergy on the conference. "I'm going to leave the Methodist church, Jennifer. I plan to get a nursing job so I can be free to live like I want to live, like I deserve to live. I like women, Jennifer, and it's causing me a lot of trouble to pretend that is not so. I hope you won't think less of me. But you need to know the truth about me."

"I love you Mama and I'm not really surprised to hear that you like women. I don't know why, but I'm not surprised."

My mind was made up. I was coming out of the closet so I could fall in love with a woman who would fall in love with me.

# COMING OUT

Through connections at the seminary, I was given three phone numbers, contacts with other women who were lesbians and Methodist ministers. I chatted with each one of them, asking how they managed their lives. I wondered if maybe I had made a mistake by saying I was leaving the Methodists. I loved serving my congregations. I was gifted for church leadership. Maybe I should ask other women how they got by in the system. I learned that the three women I spoke with were quiet, reserved, and able to stay in the closet. One of them had a secret lover. The other two had chosen celibacy. That was not for me.

I went to my therapy session with Elaine and asked her, "How will I meet other women like me? How will I find a lover?" Elaine knew a yoga and meditation instructor who taught classes at the University of Memphis. She thought Dan would know some lesbians, so she offered to make a call. I was more than ready to have a girlfriend. So much of my trouble was based on the simple matter that I liked women. I was giving up a lot for that simple matter. But I was sure I would be gaining even more. I wanted to be free, free from my mother's criticism, free from any church restrictions and free from my own fear of being something other than normal. Oh, how I hated to give up my quest to appear normal.

Dan knew lesbians in Memphis. And he gave phone numbers to Elaine. She explained, "This is a couple. They're already taken. But I think they might connect you with other women like you. Some of them will be single." She winked. "Good luck."

I called Angie Dagastino and Dottie Jones. They were lesbians, according to Dan. And they were lesbians who didn't mind being open about their relationship. I called Angie first. I said, "Hello. I'm Elaine. I want to meet lesbians and I think you're a lesbian, right?"

"Who is this?"

"I'm sorry. I got your name and number from Dan the meditation and yoga instructor?"

"Oh. Elaine. Yes. Dan did mention that Elaine might be calling us. So how can I help you?"

"Well, it's just that I think I am a lesbian. I mean I do like women. Anyway, I want to meet some women who will like me the same way I like them. I'm tired of straight women and their boundaries. I'm sick of falling in love with women who can't love me back."

Angie and her partner, Dottie, met me at Applebee's for dinner one night after my classes at the seminary. I have no idea what I ordered or even if I ate a thing. My entire body was tensed with fear. I felt sure that some Methodists would be eating in a booth across from us and report that I was eating with real live lesbians. I could hardly keep up with the conversation because all my energy was involved with reminding myself to breathe. I might be brave enough to step out a little, but I was feeling the weight of needing my income as a pastor and needing the assistance of the Methodist church for my seminary tuition. My paranoia was in high gear.

Angie and Dottie told me about Meristem, a bookstore for women in the Cooper-Young neighborhood. They told me about the Memphis Gay and Lesbian Center. They told me that gay people got together once a month at Calvary Episcopal Church. "They worship together, have a dinner and a program of some sort." Angie could tell I was amazed to learn that gay people could be comfortable to be who they were in a church. My head was spinning. What kind of church could that be?

I was taking a course in feminist theology at the seminary. One of the theologians we were studying was Virginia Mollenkott. I connected with her story of having endured a conservative upbringing. We were reading her book, *Sensuous Spirituality: Out From Fundamentalism.* I learned that Dr. Mollenkott was accustomed to hate mail and death threats. She was reported to have said, "There are some things worth dying for." I wrote to Dr. Mollenkott, mailing the letter to her publisher, Crossroad Publishing Company. I asked Dr. Mollenkott if she had a partner and told her, if not, I would be interested. I told her that I didn't know any lesbians in my area. She wrote back to me, thanking me for my compliments and for my interest. She told me she had a partner, and she knew lesbians in Memphis who would welcome me into their lives. She gave me a phone number for Jane Hampshire and Le Martin, two Catholic women, who had been together as partners for many years. I called them and they invited Jennifer and me to have dinner with them. They became good friends to both of us.

Emily Matheny, a seminary friend, stood outside the student center one morning and said, "You know, you probably need an accountant friend or a CPA. If you're leaving a marriage where gambling has been an issue, you might want to get a good look at what your finances are doing." She had a business card ready for me: Raynor Shoaf. I made an appointment to meet with this accountant. I took my tax information and a huge need to be heard. Raynor listened. She paid attention to my fears about where I might be as a single woman without a parsonage. I knew that creditors were calling us constantly about Doug's debts. I didn't know where I could go or if I could afford to divorce Doug. I had been willing to let Doug manage our money, and I knew I was going to pay dearly for that error in judgement.

I just needed to know how to get started being smarter for myself and for Jennifer's sake. Raynor was a calming influence and I appreciated her.

That night I tried to study for my Worship and Preaching class, but I kept thinking about Raynor. She wore a fanny pack, her hair was cut very short, and her Polo shirt was tucked into her carpenter pants. She had a male swagger when she walked around the corner of her desk to greet me. I began to wonder if Raynor might be lesbian and maybe that's why Emily had given me her card. So, with my daughter at the other end of the house and nobody else around to judge me, I called Raynor's number.

"Hello?"

"This is Elaine, the one who came to your office today?"

"Sure. Is there a problem?"

"No, no problem. I was just wondering if maybe, well I wanted to ask you if you are lesbian."

"Let me close the door," she said. Then there was a pause. "Before I answer your question, I need to know will the answer to that question affect your doing business with me?"

"No. No. I am asking because I want to get to know some lesbians. And I wonder if you are one?"

"Why are you wanting to know some other lesbians, Elaine?"

"I have been keeping my desire a secret for a long time and now I'm wanting to meet someone who will love me the way I love her."

"Let's have lunch," Raynor offered. I learned that she had her own girlfriend. But she was more than willing to introduce me to some of her friends. She gave me a phone number for her friend. I called the number, and I liked Connie, Connie Blaylock. She was a nurse. So, we arranged to get together and go to the riverside for Memphis in May Music Festival. Turned out, Raynor's family-owned property in Ripley, where Jennifer was attending high school. That was Raynor's old stomping grounds. She and her friends came to sit with me at Jennifer's graduation from high school. They didn't want me to be alone. Doug and his family sat apart from me. That was the night I gave up pretending to be anything I am not. I was being embraced in a new family of friends and I felt safe for the first time in a long time.

One day during my seminary training a man named Ed Loring came to the seminary and had lunch with anyone who wanted to hear about his work among the unhoused citizens of Atlanta. Ed's booming voice told us about The Open Door, a place of hospitality on Ponce De Leon Avenue, for those who have no permanent address. Ed was recruiting students to volunteer for an internship at The Open Door. I raised my hand immediately. I was hungry to do something new and different. Changes were happening inside me and I wanted to change my circumstances a bit. See myself in a new situation.

On the first of July, 1993, a very hot day, I packed my car and drove to Atlanta where I was given a room in the basement, next to the pantry. Every guest and intern at The Open Door had to live by three house rules. 1.) Show respect to everyone in the house 2.) Report to the daily house manager when you are leaving the house and tell him or her when you plan to return. 3.) Do your daily assigned chores. Those seemed like simple rules, but they were challenging for some guests, especially those with active addictions and untreated mental health problems. If a person was unable to keep the rules, then they could not live inside the house. Many unhoused neighbors lived in the side and back yards of The Open Door. They were beloved members of the community whether they could keep the rules or not. We served breakfast every morning at Butler Street Christian Methodist Episcopal (CME) Church. We made a huge vat of coffee with milk in it, and we served grits, boiled eggs and orange slices to hundreds of hungry people who lined up on the street. We also provided multiple vitamins to those who came through the line.

One morning I was handing out vitamins when a man stepped up to receive his pill and I glanced at him, a black man who seemed to wear the weight of the world on his bent shoulders. His face was half covered by the dark hoodie he wore. I handed Him the vitamin, and he touched my hand, saying "Thanks" in a low tone. I was moved, as if I had just served Jesus himself. I felt a divine presence in that moment and in that man's spirit. That exchange changed me, changed the way I saw others, as I came to realize the face of Christ in all my neighbors. It changed my awareness of my own divinity, my own internal image of God. I am a lesbian and I am who God created me to be. I am not a mistake or a problem. I learned that lesson while living at The Open Door.

The internship lasted a month, keeping me busy with making food, serving food, doing laundry and handing out clean clothes and sneakers. Work is never ending, and it became more and more meaningful to me. We did some resting and enjoying ourselves. One day a large group of us went to a movie. I don't remember what movie we saw but I do recall how much fun we had walking to the theatre and back. We stopped for ice cream on our walk home. Another day I drove to the beach near Savannah. I took my German neighbor, Ute, with me to the beach. She was interning from

Frankfurt. One day we went to the courthouse and sat in a courtroom, escaping the outside July heat. And other days we went to the public library where we read books and enjoyed the publicly available air-conditioned temperature. The Open Door is not air conditioned because closing the windows and cooling the inside air would mean further shutting out the neighbors who live in the yard. The rule of hospitality required that we be able to hear the voices of those who lived outside. I brought home cards and artwork made by the community members. I walked away from that internship so much richer than I had arrived.

On June 9, 1994, Jennifer and I moved to Memphis. My therapist, Elaine, was on stand-by. A convoy of pick-up trucks, members of my congregations, wanted to help with my move, moving everything Jennifer and I owned from the parsonage in Gates to the big city of Memphis. It stormed terribly that day; sheets of rain pummeled the trucks and their tarps. I had been warned; several friends urged me not to move during the storm. But I was ready to get free and I was not interested in waiting. The kind church members, all men, took the lightning and claps of thunder as an adventure. I lost one pair of Sunday short heels in a ditch along the way. Everything else made it to our new home on Cox Street in the Cooper-Young neighborhood where being gay was normal.

I had a job at St Francis Hospital. Jennifer had a scholarship to attend the University of Memphis. I would be nobody's pastor. We would experience life without feeling the need to hide our money and checkbooks because Doug no longer lived with us. I would no longer need to hide my feelings for women. Ours would be a very, very, very fine house.

We moved into a duplex that belonged to my new girlfriend, Connie, the nurse Raynor had introduced to me. We were getting along just fine, talking on the phone and meeting between Memphis and Gates for dinners at truck stops and fast-food joints. Then one night, after my classes and after dinner at Applebee's, we went back to Connie's place, and we took off our clothes. It happened slowly and easily. Then we were both hungrily kissing one another and reaching for sensitive body parts. We were a couple after that afternoon, an item in the minds of all our friends and in our own minds.

Jennifer went off to her college classes each morning; she had her own car. And I went off to the day shift on the alcohol and drug treatment unit at St. Francis Hospital. I felt fortunate to land a day-shift job. I had to start early, 6:45 in the morning, but I was off work while the sun was still shining and time for me to engage in romance. I liked my work, helping patients accept their powerlessness. It helped me to stay in touch with my own weaknesses and failures. I was certain that abstinence from alcohol was giving me strength

176

to pull a new life together. I found a gay AA group, *Seriously Sober,* where I connected with new friends.

Jennifer and I started attending First Congregational United Church of Christ in Midtown. My Christology and New Testament professor, Dr. Ron Cole-Turner, suggested I give that church a try. "I think you'll feel at home there," he had assured me. I trusted him. And he was right. The preacher, Rev. Cheryl Cornish, preached interesting sermons, sermons that made me think, and the space itself was traditional and comfortable. Because I had heard that gay people were welcome there, I was afraid the building and its sanctuary might be outlandish, colorful tacky banners and flamboyant paraments instead of straight forward pews with a pulpit up front. I found the traditional sanctuary a comfort.

One Sunday in August, during the coffee hour, when people wandered about and got to know each other, I introduced myself to a tall, red-headed woman. She was freckled and there was an ease about her that spoke of great confidence. She told me her name was Darlene. I asked her what she did for work.

"I am on faculty at Rhodes College," she said as she popped a carrot into her mouth.

"What do you teach?"

"English literature and writing courses."

I reached across the table to get a cookie, and Darlene quickly picked it up and handed it to me. Her smile was wide and wonderful as she watched me put the cookie to my lips. She could see that I was altogether impressed. Her eyes sparkled and I recognized the invitation there. We went to Overton Park and walked together around Rainbow Lake. Then we went to her house where we made love as if it would be our last chance ever to get good loving. Darlene became my second girlfriend.

Being in a relationship with Darlene introduced me to the faculty at Rhodes College. A group of them enjoyed *Grill and Chill* every Friday night at one house or another. Darlene and I never missed those fun times. I got to know professors who taught Spanish, women's studies, religion, math, biology, and psychology. Because I had my ex-husband's gambling debts to pay off, I started a pet-sitting business, a way to add to my income as a nurse. My new Rhodes friends hired me to walk their dogs and see to their houses when they were away. My side business took off and I settled in to being part of the academic community. I paid off debts and looked forward to the divorce being final.

Darlene and I sat next to each other at church every Sunday during worship. We both volunteered to be on a support team, Regional AIDS Interfaith Network. As volunteers, we assisted gay men who were dying with AIDS, men who had no family to be with them while they died. We acted as family. Making food, reading out loud, playing music, watching television. We changed the bed and washed clothes toward the end of each life. It was meaningful for me. It was ministry.

The relationship with Darlene lasted a couple of years. They were good years, full of healing and fun times. But I wasn't ready to be fully committed. I was still trying to find myself.

# ALMA

F riends helped me move into The Rosecrest, a high-rise, where I rented a place on the fourth floor. Meg Jones helped me haul a new futon into the elevator and down the hall. I bought a used table and chairs set. Then I spent real money on a twin bed. With a good coffee maker, I was settled in and comfortable. The apartment came with a refrigerator, stove, and microwave. Paintings and various fun stuff like lamps could wait until the next paycheck.

One rainy Thursday night, I was on my way home to my apartment after a day at work and a couple of dog walking gigs. I turned left to cross two lanes of traffic and only one lane stopped for me. It was a bad crash but the other driver and I survived. We walked away in good shape. No broken bones, miraculously. Both cars were totaled. Seat belts really do save lives. I was sore the next day with seat belt burns across my chest. Even so, I had to go to work. But I had no car.

I called my pastor, Cheryl, and told her I had had an accident. My car had been towed away. And I needed a ride to work and back until I figured out what to do. We had a close-knit circle of women friends in the church. Cheryl made a call, and I had a ride waiting for me at 6:30 the following morning. Tiger, a homeless lesbian who lived in her truck, was interested in giving me rides back and forth to St Francis Hospital. For as many days as I needed her, Tiger was on time every morning and waiting in her truck outside the hospital every afternoon. Until Raynor gave me a ride out to the car lots on Covington Pike, where I bought a pick-up truck of my own. I liked the look of being butch in a pick-up. And I liked the idea of being able to return some favors. I had been the recipient of lots of pick-up truck moves.

My work life was stable while so many things changed as I settled into lesbian life in Memphis. I worked the day shift, Monday through Friday, on the alcohol and drug treatment unit at St Francis Hospital. Alma, the charge nurse on the midnight shift, was always glad to see me and glad to leave. Alma was beyond retirement age but, for financial reasons, she couldn't retire. She blamed her situation on a husband who had gone out one night to get a pack of cigarettes and never returned home. "He just disappeared," Alma explained. She was a born-again Christian. Alma brought a big Bible to work with her and she read it while she sat at the nurses' station during the night. She believed that alcoholism and drug addiction were clear signs of moral weakness and a lack of self-discipline. When patients called for a nurse and requested medication, Alma suggested that they pray and ask God for relief. She gave the patients Bible verses to read.

"Just praise the Lord for all he's done for you," she urged the patients, "and the act of praise will relieve you of your headache."

Alma was not a favorite among the nurses or among the patients. Regularly we dealt with complaints about how the night had gone. One morning I came to work, and I found the entire community of patients in an uproar. Apparently during the night, a man had been admitted who was positive for HIV. Alma had put him in a room at the end of the hall and she had sat in the doorway of his room while she filled out his admission papers. The man was not bleeding from any orifice, nor was he interested in engaging in any sexual activity with Alma. But he did get sick during Alma's shift. He vomited and Alma moved him to another room. She pushed towels on the floor up against the door of his original room and put duct-tape around the door to seal it. She called housekeeping and then went back to reading her Bible.

I was told that the new admission started feeling better as the sun rose and he came out of his room and walked toward the breakfast buffet, a table set up in the hallway. Orange juice, coffee, sweet rolls and cereals, bananas and apples were set out for everyone to enjoy. But Alma looked up from her reading in time to head the new man off. "Oh no," she jumped up and wagged her finger. "You can't eat from this table. You take your HIV and get back in your room."

"What do you think, Alma?" another patient caught the scene as he walked out of his room. "Do you think the man is going to have sex on the buffet table or is he just wanting a cup of java?" About that time several other patients came out of their rooms and there was much laughter and many high-fives as the new man introduced himself and helped himself to coffee. By the time I arrived at work, the boom box was blaring, and everyone was having a good time. Everyone, that is, except for Alma.

She gave report to our oncoming shift and warned us that the new admission was positive for HIV. "There's nothing we need to do differently for him than what we would do for any other patient," I reminded Alma that we used universal precautions on all patients. "There's nothing to worry about," I touched her shoulder as a gesture of reassurance. But she slapped my hand off her shoulder with a snarl.

"Just because you live with the sin of homosexuality doesn't mean the rest of us need to normalize your perversion." She stood up. "And keep your hands off of me."

# WOMYN'S MUSIC FESTIVAL

On December 9, 1994, I went to court with my attorney and was declared legally divorced. Doug didn't show up and he hadn't contested the divorce. But he did agree to meet me at a Shoney's Restaurant in Millington, where he returned my journals. It was all I wanted from him.

I started looking for a new love focus. I had given up so much for the sake of my sexuality and I wasn't getting younger. I was forty-two years old and just beginning to get comfortable with my new identity as a lesbian. I needed to move along with finding a new partner. Being alone was not exciting enough and I could have stayed with the Methodists if I was willing to live without romance in my life.

I was attracted to Sarah Douglas, a nurse practitioner who worked at St Jude. She was smart and fun and very comfortable with herself. Her faith, she was a devout Catholic, meant a great deal to her. I knew her through mutual friends in the recovery community. I invited her to my apartment for coffee and cookies one night after a12-Step meeting. She sat on my futon, and we chatted. Sarah told me about her only sibling, a brother, who was highly successful in his military career. She was obviously very proud of her brother. I got up to make coffee and called to her from the kitchen, "So how did your brother react when you told him you are gay?"

"Oh," she called back from her spot in the living room, "I'm not gay."

I dropped the measuring spoon on the floor and lost count of the scoops of coffee I was dumping into the filter. "You're not?" This woman had all the earmarks of a lesbian. She dressed in sports jackets and turtle-neck shirts. Her shoes were comfortable, and her hair was short. She was unmarried and professional. And she attended 12-Step meetings that were primarily for gay and lesbian people. I couldn't believe I had misread the signs.

"No. I've just never married." She was gracious about my mistake. But after that, the coffee and cookies seemed rather pointless to me. I had been interested in something more.

My regular AA group met every Friday night at 8:00, and we followed the meeting with eating together at TGI Friday's on the Square. Most of us were gay which made everything feel safe and fun. We had plenty to laugh about and we were serious about guarding our recovery. We were a support system for each other. I started looking for a love object in our group.

"If I were looking for a girlfriend," Timothy considered, "I would check out Samantha Collins. She has a lot going for her." And I moved closer to Samantha, choosing to sit beside her every Friday night at the AA meetings, and sitting next to her when we got seated at Friday's. She had a hearty laugh, and she thought I was funny. She laughed at my stories. She was several years younger than I and she was an art therapist. I liked the entire package. I invited her to see a movie with me, *Men in Black*. We had a nice time.

My therapist at the time was Lynn Bergeron and she was helping me fully celebrate the legal divorce from my marriage. She urged me to stay single and unattached long enough to experience being me without the obvious complications that come with a sexual relationship. I didn't listen. I pursued Samantha. She belonged to a group of lesbians who liked to go out in the woods together where they built bonfires and engaged in ancient rituals, celebrating the stages of being a woman and becoming a crone.

A group of us went to the Michigan Womyn's Music Festival. As we drove onto the grounds, we were greeted by strong looking women who came to the car window and said, "Welcome home." We parked the car on a grassy field and started unloading our camping gear into a wagon: a tent, sleeping bags, blankets, pillows, clothes, snacks water jugs, Frisbees, journals, art supplies and sex toys. The festival is protected by volunteer guards who patrol the perimeter, making sure no men come onto the property during the week-long event. Special areas were designated for younger women with children, young women without children, smokers, partying women, older women, quiet women, recovering women, nude women, muscle building women and sado-masochistic women. The first day was given over to settling in, pitching tents, and gathering wood for fire pits. And then came the opening ceremony. The Indigo Girls, Alanis Morissette, and so many other talented musicians were performing their hearts out on a huge stage while enormous and brightly colored puppets filled the sky around us all. They walked from the back of the crowd, as we were sitting on a grassy hillside, down the hill to the stage. Giant balloons towered over us all. The music had us swaying for hours. When darkness covered us, we walked by the light of our flashlights back to our camp space and crawled into our tents.

Everyone showered in the same open field. A long pipe stretched about thirty feet across the grassy ground. There were showerheads every three feet. We lined up in the nude and held our soap, shampoo, and towel, waiting our turn to get showered. After I took my first shower, I gained the courage to join so many others who had left our clothes in a duffle bag, to be put back on when we headed out for the return trip outside *The Land*. I realized my body was not something to be ashamed of. My belly isn't as flat as I wish it were, and I have felt embarrassed about the bulge. And there's all the trauma I still carry from the abuse I suffered as a child.

But at the Womyn's Festival, I let go of all that discomfort with my body. There were so many of us going without clothes. Some women were large with roll upon roll of abdomen under huge breasts, some women were so muscular and beefy, some were thin as rails, angular and bony, and some of them had beards as well as hairy arms and legs. I felt free. I have never felt safer. It was a secure experience along with being exciting, a lovely combination. Sex was excellent during the festival. Samantha and I looked forward to bedtime. Our imaginations were well fed.

The only time men were allowed on the property were the over-night occasions when the porta-potties had to be emptied. The sewer crew was guarded carefully by volunteers from the muscle-building section. The men were counted at the gate as they entered *The Land* and heads were counted at the gate when the sewer crew departed just before sun rise.

We all ate together. Food was served under one huge tent. Every woman participated in the work of preparing food and cleaning up after meals. Assignments were given upon entry into the festival so that there were no surprises. From the start, each one of us knew when we were expected to show up and invest our time and skill in making meals happen. There were no paper plates or napkins allowed. Each woman brought her own plate, cloth napkin and utensils to the table and each woman washed her own plate and utensils after each meal.

The vendors in the marketplace sold original art, clothing, musical instruments, books, jewelry, snacks, sex toys and tools. Workshops taught us how to wear the clothing and how to use the toys and tools. My favorite moment of the entire week was the opportunity to meet Alice Walker who read from her book, *The Same River Twice*. She signed my copy of *The Color Purple,* and she encouraged me as a writer. It was a moment I'll never forget, standing naked in front of Alice Walker. "Don't give up. Keep writing and keep sending your work out there. It will find the place where it belongs." She had her clothes on.

There was no pressure for any camper to go naked. It was a choice each one of us made on our own. It was the first time I ever internalized the idea that all bodies are beautiful. None of us got to choose the body we were given. It is the container that holds our life. And it deserves to be well treated and loved. I found myself loving my stride as I hiked through the woods, loving my hands as they washed huge pots and pans, loving my mouth as it kissed Samantha, long and lustful kisses with the outdoor breeze caressing us. Most amazing of all, I loved my belly, the part of me that I had always felt was most hateful. It always seemed to say, "I'm not who I ought to be." But during the Michigan Festival, I fell in love with every bit of my wild, soft body. The love in the food that fed me there was delicious.

After the festival, I explained to my therapist, Liz, that I had to leave Samantha. No matter what I said, she feared I would leave her. So, I finally did. It was the only option she left available for peace. Or maybe I was just ready to try someone new. Whatever the interior motivations, I moved into a back house in the city's historic Evergreen District. Linda and Hutch Dickerson, friends at the church, cleaned out their back house and invited me to live in it, rent free, with the only obligation being paying the utilities and pet sitting for them when they traveled.

I was in a full-time educational and professional chaplaincy program at Methodist Hospital, Clinical Pastoral Education. I had decided, during my therapy sessions with Liz, that the thing I most wanted out of my life was the opportunity to continue my journey toward ordained ministry. I knew I was gifted for the calling. I was now part of a church and a denomination, the United Church of Christ, an institution that ordained gay and lesbian and transgender people. I was free to follow my call. I went back to Memphis Theological Seminary to finish my course requirements to earn an M.Div. And I enrolled in the CPE program where Sue Beverly was the supervisor.

Sue became my therapist and eventually, one of my closest friends. A tiny woman, no more than a hundred pounds at her heaviest, she was vain. It took her two hours every morning to fix her hair and makeup for an ordinary day at the hospital. She was picky about her eating. Her lunch each day was a skinless roasted chicken breast and a boiled egg. She took a palmful of supplements which had been recommended to her by her licensed herbalist. She spent time several days a week in the tanning bed. Sue had an eye for bullshit. She could see it coming. So those of us who were in her class as resident-chaplains had to be up front and honest or be called out loudly in front of the class.

Our mornings were spent seeing patients in our assigned area of the hospital, and our afternoons were spent in group therapy sessions. We talked about our faith, our families, our values, and our personal issues. The point of the program was to make us a strong support for people dealing with hospitalization. Some of the other students thought the point of the program was to appear more pious than anybody else.

For those more pious ones, Sue had no mercy. I loved Sue. I loved her for who she was, and for the tough questions she asked in one-on-one sessions and in the group. I loved her for her courage and her sense of humor. I also loved how irreverent she could be. Sitting in worship stimulated her anxiety disorder. So, she rapidly tapped her forehead and wrists when we sat in chapel each morning.

My area was the Emergency Room at Le Bonheur, the children's hospital. I was called to be a support when children were admitted with broken bones or when a child passed away. As the chaplain, I showed up and offered spiritual support by my presence and prayers. I did my best to build rapport and trust but those were high goals in a small room where a child's life had been snuffed out by a gunshot or a four-wheel accident. The pain was palpable. And I was a stranger who prayed. It felt to me that the words I said were significant so I chose my words carefully.

"What did you say to give them some reassurance, some hope?" Sue leaned over, her elbows on her knees.

"I said, would you like prayer?"

"So, you punted the ball. You guarded yourself, just avoided being real with those hurting human beings by stepping back and offering prayer. What are you so afraid of? What are you afraid those people will see if you offer them something real? What were you feeling in that room?"

"I was afraid."

"Ok." She slapped her knee. "Of what?"

"I was afraid I didn't have anything to offer those people. They were moaning and crying with anguish. I felt like a stranger dropped into their family, like I didn't belong."

"You didn't belong," Sue scoffed and rolled her eyes back in head. Then with full force, "You were sent there to provide a service, to offer spiritual support. You didn't need to be their sister or friend. You had a job to do. Please tell me your prayer was a comfort to these suffering souls."

It was Sue who introduced me to my new therapist, Mark Winborn. Sue was part of a Jungian Study Group and so was Dr. Winborn, a Jungian psychoanalyst. He deals with dreams, symbols, and stories. I started seeing Dr. Winborn and struggling with my call to ministry that could and would interfere with my romantic life. If I wanted to serve a church in the United Church of Christ denomination, I would have to leave Memphis. The Memphis options were taken; all of the local congregations had pastors. I put my profile out across the United States. And I talked with Dr. Winborn about the congregations who responded positively to my profile, wanting to know more about me. I was glad for his help in discernment. And I was happy to talk about my new love, a woman I met at church.

# ANNA

While I was considering where I might land as a local church pastor, I was falling in love with Anna Neal. It all began in 1998, when Anna visited our church as the guest pianist. She played two beautiful pieces and I liked looking at her as she played. I could feel a surge of passion coming from her body to my body through my ears and the waves of music that she played. She brought the piano to life in me and all of us. I felt a deep attraction to her.

Anna came back to our church, not as a guest musician but as a visitor. She joined a group of us who met for lunch after worship each week. We all gathered around a big table at The Cupboard, a down-home place where we could get a meat and three sides, homecooked vegetables with corn bread. Always there was peach or apple cobbler. We liked to laugh at that table. We laughed, telling one story after another about our lives and our jobs and our struggles. I loved to talk about being a seminary student and a resident chaplain. I told stories and Anna laughed. She was entertained by me, and I found that endearing. A beautiful woman, Anna was also smart. A music librarian, she knew a lot and I was impressed.

We both volunteered to help with a 5-K Run to benefit the Women's Rape and Resource Center. The race was called

*Take Back the Night*. I knew that night, as I handed out cups of water to the runners, that Anna was meant for me. She came by and I handed her a cup of water and watched her walk away. I liked what I saw.

Around Thanksgiving, Anna called me and asked me if I would like to have coffee after our church's pilgrim performance. All of us Congregationalists dressed up as pilgrim men and women and walked solemnly and slowly to the beat of a drum. We walked from the back of the church around to the front steps. We walked up the stairs and into the sanctuary, women seated on one side and men on the other. The sermon was bullying and accusatory. Members of the congregation were brought up before the group and publicly shamed. It was all theater and the back of the church was full of people who had simply come to see the show. We pretended to be the Seventeenth Century pilgrims who landed on the shore of the Atlantic on Plymouth Rock. We sat in our pews and looked alert lest the man with the feather and nob stick come by and either tickle our noses with the feather or bop our skulls with the nob. It was all great fun, a bonding experience for those of us who participated. Anna and I went to Starbucks for coffee afterward. I was glad to be single and glad to move closer to that piano playing woman.

"You're a librarian at the university?" I asked as we got seated with our lattes.

"I'm the music librarian there, and I supervise the branch libraries."

"That sounds like a lot of work. Do you enjoy what you do?"

"I do. Most of the time. But I am not very good at the supervision part of my job. I hate being the one who does the supervising, checking up on people and writing their evaluations. It's not my strong point."

"What is your strong point?"

"Oh, I have no idea. What's your strong point?"

"I am flexible; I adapt quickly to change."

"Why do you think that is?"

"Oh, I don't know. It's a skill I developed when I was very young, being transferred from one house to another while my mother was sick with tuberculosis. I learned to be at home wherever. Tell me what your strong point is."

"I'm loyal and I stay well informed," she answered after more thought.

I carried all the warm, fuzzy feelings to therapy with Mark. I really hoped Anna turned out to be gay. I hadn't heard her say the words. And I knew from experience, that all the signs can point toward gay, and I could pick up on it. But not everybody is ready to be responded to that way. I waited on Anna to make it clear to me.

She called me and invited me to dinner at a local spot and then to go see the movie, *The Green Mile* with Tom Hanks. We ate vegetarian at La Montaigne, and shared some terrific multi-grain bread. Then we sat through a movie side by side. There was some body heat exchanged leg to leg. But no hand holding. I still wasn't sure whether we were friends or potential lovers. And it's so costly to make a mistake about that. I continued to wait for a word from Anna. When we parted ways, there was a moment when a kiss might have been in order. But since there had been no word of reassurance, I simply shook her hand with a perfunctory yank, and said, "I had a good time." She started grinning and I was lost in embarrassment. I got out of the car and felt like a complete idiot, "Big dummy! Big dummy!" The signs were all there. But I was so afraid of making a mistake.

Anna paged me one day when I was on duty at the hospital. I took a break and called her back. She said, "I've made some chicken noodle soup. It's pretty good if I do say so myself. When you get hungry for lunch, why don't you come by and have some soup with me?"

When I got off my chaplaincy shift, I hustled hungrily to Anna's house. I felt confident that this invitation had to do with more than just chicken soup. There was something big in this and I drove while grinning from the medical center all the way to east Memphis. I was not wrong. She liked me like that. And I returned the feeling. And we made a connection that thrilled us both. We made a commitment to each other after we ate the soup.

I told her that I wanted to be loyal to a relationship, but I hadn't yet found the right one. She said, "Let's see if this turns out to be what you're looking for." We attended a Christmas party that night at Joel and Gary's place, friends from our church. It was clear that we were a new item. Our friends were all so happy for us. It was fresh and tender, but it felt like forever would not be long enough to bask in this kind of solid trustworthy love.

I was involved in a search and call process as a minister. For a few weeks, it looked like I would be going to Gilman, Iowa to serve Gilman Community Church. I met with the search committee and we had a wonderful time together, feeling as though we were led by the Holy Spirit. We planned for the congregation to meet me in person, have a chance to connect with me personally and then I would tell them that I was in a committed relationship with a woman, Anna. But one member of the search committee told her husband, "That woman we're considering for our new pastor is a lesbian." And her husband told his sister, and the sister called her best friend. As a result, an angry group of people disrupted worship the Sunday before I was to meet with the congregation. They read scripture from Romans and Leviticus. And they threatened to remove their financial support if the search committee proceeded with calling a lesbian to be their pastor. I chose to drop out of their process, even though it had felt so right to those of us who were involved. I didn't think I could deal with the hostility. Sue Beverly and my therapist both supported my decision to keep looking for a church that would be a good fit for me and for the congregation. The Gilman, Iowa search committee felt badly about what had happened. They traveled as a group to Memphis and attended my graduation from Memphis Theological Seminary.

Sixth Avenue United Church of Christ in Denver, Colorado seemed to be the right place for me. They were already an Open and Affirming congregation, meaning that they had already decided as a group to be a welcoming place for GLBTQ people. The search committee called me to be their pastor, and they came to Memphis for my ordination service on September 10, 2000.

Anna and I packed things in my pickup truck, along with my little dog, Sophie, and we drove to Denver. Anna would continue to live in Memphis, but our plan was to regularly travel back and forth, sustaining a long-distance relationship. It started snowing as we arrived in Denver, so we drove to

Target where we bought a hat and gloves for both of us. Adjusting to the mile high environment and the Midwest culture had begun. "Always carry an extra layer of clothing in your car," the church folks taught me. The weather in Denver could go from summer to winter in an afternoon.

The congregation celebrated my arrival in Colorado. A reception was held at a church member's home. I was embraced over and over, and words of appreciation were shared. I moved into a small apartment by Cheesman Park. Sophie and I took our daily walk through the park. I was given a desktop computer to use in my home and another to use in my office at the church. I enjoyed preaching for a liberal congregation. I got involved with social justice work on Capitol Hill and got to know other clergy in the city. It seemed like a dream job.

What I hadn't considered was how lonely I would be, so far away from Jennifer, Anna, and my Memphis friends. On Sundays, following worship, people shook my hand, told me they appreciated the message and then they all went to various places for lunch. I was accustomed to having Sunday lunch with Jennifer, Anna, and our church group. But I was neither family nor friend in Denver. I was the pastor and although no one intentionally excluded me from their lunch plans, it was not the custom to invite the pastor home for Sunday dinner. Eating alone after church brought tears to my eyes. I was homesick.

I was busy enough with my work so that I didn't feel the effect of missing home constantly. But when my authority as pastor was challenged by a church member, a young man who gave generously to the church finances, I was not prepared emotionally to deal with the conflict. I started drinking again after seventeen years of sobriety. And at the same time, I allowed myself to be pulled into a power struggle that I could not win. I drank alone, talking to Anna on the phone at night.

I started hanging out socially with a couple of lesbians who had a longstanding grudge against the church. Their negative energy and my neediness were not a healthy mixture. Instead of leading the congregation, I found myself becoming a divisive entity. And then the planes flew into the Twin Towers in New York City. All of us were frightened. I did my best to comfort a congregation that was beginning to question my appropriateness as their pastor. My best friend in Denver, Phil Campbell, was a big help. He walked with me in the park and listened to my ongoing struggles. A clergy person, Phil understood what I was going through, and his support gave me strength. In talking with him, I realized that I wanted more than anything to go home. Denying that, and trying to avoid my homesickness, was only causing problems for me and for the church. On December 18, 2001, Anna and I packed my things, and we drove back to Tennessee.

# MOM

I'd like to say that I learned my lesson, that I stayed with Anna and Jennifer in Memphis, stopped drinking too much, and found work right there at home. But I didn't do that. I took a course on managing church conflict through the Alban Institute. I got a therapist who met with me weekly to help me grow emotionally. And I accepted a call to move to Birmingham, only a five-hour drive from Memphis, where I served Pilgrim Congregational Church for one year. I was no better prepared to deal with the conflicts in Birmingham than I had been in Denver. Pilgrim Congregational had a maintenance man, who was also a member of the church. I confronted him about his attitude toward me and lost the struggle. I created division again. In March of 2003, I moved back to Memphis and took a job as a registered nurse on a neurosurgery floor at the hospital. It paid so much better than preaching. I tried to focus on the positive, but I felt like a failure.

My mother deteriorated quickly after her husband died in 2004. None of us had seen how the two of them held each other up. When he died, Mom slumped in body and in spirit and she began to fall. At one point, she broke her right arm and couldn't take care of herself, so she came to stay with me in Birmingham while her arm healed. We had long talks and the two of us ironed out so many past troubles. We cleared the air in our relationship.

Returned to her own retirement apartment, she continued to fall, smacking her head against hard surfaces, breaking bones and creating a stir among her neighbors who were also retired faculty from Trevecca Nazarene College. The neighbors, though good friends, grew understandably weary with picking up my mother from the floor in various rooms of her apartment, calling emergency services and then accompanying her to the emergency room where they sat and felt useless for hours. Drell and Jerry Allen called me and explained their frustration and fear. Mom was unable to care for herself. She had flooded her apartment by leaving the kitchen faucet on over a plugged sink and letting it run all night long. It made sense to me that someone in the family needed to take care of Mom. When I called my three brothers, they all agreed that I should be the one to go get Mom and plan for her safety. Anna became my right hand in all that went into caring for a demented woman who was physically strong and willful, denying that she needed any kind of assistance. I drove to Nashville and brought Mom home to Memphis, to live with Anna and me. Mom loved Anna and she enjoyed living with us. We hired a sitter to stay with her while I worked the evening shift at the hospital.

Mom fell in the bathroom one night, hitting her face against the sink and countertop, breaking her mandible and the orbital bones around her eye. The poor dear looked like a monster and that fall took something out of her spirit. She curled up in a fetal position and stayed that way unless she was forced to turn over or sit up. I took her to a neuro-psychologist for testing. But Mom wasn't alert enough to engage in the testing. My purpose in taking her was to find out if she had a blood clot on her brain due to her many falls. But the doctors all said it was simple dementia.

For six years she laid in bed at St Peter's Manor. She would eat only when fed. She wore diapers. There were days she could speak and days when she could not speak at all. I paid her bills and looked after her business. I visited her every day, laundering her clothes, and checking on her personal hygiene, and connecting with the aides who were assigned to her care. She fell out of bed twice, each time breaking a bone. Those incidents required that I leave work and meet the ambulance at the hospital's emergency department. The pain and disruption made her cry. Parked for hours on a stretcher in the hallway of the emergency area, she cried, and I stood by her side, patting her, and doing my best to reassure her. She was too frail for surgery. The ER doctor taped a pillow to her broken femur and sent her back to St Peter's.

In 2010, while I was filing my mother's nails, I saw her eyes light up. "I know you," she cooed, her head tilted to one side.

"I know you too," I grinned, delighted to hear her voice.

"You're that little girl who used to crawl around my bed when I was sick with TB. You made animal noises, moo-moo, quack quack, trying to make me laugh. Yes, I remember you."

"If you say so. I don't remember, but it sounds like me." I brushed her hair back from her face and looked into her eyes. "What else do you remember?"

"You're that little girl who got that black boy out of jail."

"What?"

"Yes!" She was excited. Leaning forward and pointing at me, "You're the little girl who refused to identify that black boy. And the police had no choice but to let him go free. Turned him loose. Yes. I remember you."

# CHAPTER V

## BECOMING A PLAYWRIGHT

Brooks Ramsey became my spiritual guide and counselor. A man the same age as my mother, Brooks had been a Southern Baptist preacher. But when he marched in Memphis with Dr. Martin Luther King Jr. and the sanitation workers, who were striking for safe working conditions, his church fired him. Following that, Brooks went back to school and got his doctorate in pastoral counseling. Brooks understood church conflict and he became a source of healing and hope for me. We met each week in his home and he had a way of helping me find what was true and good within me. I described my shame at how poorly I had managed my affairs in Denver and in Birmingham. But Brooks saw me as a survivor, strong and capable. "You've got enthusiasm!" he reminded me. "You are creative and exuberant!" He read poetry to me and prayed with me until I came to believe in myself again.

I started hosting clergy women gatherings at my home each month, inviting local clergy women to come by on Friday afternoons to have refreshments and to support each other. Sharon Oglesby joined us, along with Gail Gaddie and Emily Matheny and other clergy friends. It was a chance to reconnect and encourage each other. Sharon was retired and no longer felt threatened by our friendship. I was in a stable relationship with my partner, Anna, and no longer felt attracted to other women. We found ourselves free to be friends again.

One Sunday afternoon Anna and I were at the theater seeing a matinee and, on the way out, I picked up a post card that advertised a series of playwriting workshops to be held by a local theater group, *Voices of the South*. "Hey, Anna," I said as we walked out to the car, "this is what I'll do. I'm going to register for these workshops and write a play about what happened to that black boy in the field."

A group of writers met in the auditorium of a private school for girls. During the first workshop we sat in a circle and told our stories. I told the group about Mack, a black man I had known when I was a child. Mack did work for white people, mowing lawns, washing cars, raking leaves, changing the oil in cars. I thought Mack could do anything. He always wore a brown sports coat and held his hat in his hands when he knocked on our back door. "Any work for me today, ma'am?" he asked my mother. She had him gather pecans from the trees in our back yard and sometimes he burned trash for us. Mama made lunch for both of us, bologna sandwiches. She made coffee for Mack and Kool Aid for me. I sat on the back steps and ate my lunch next to Mack, telling him everything I knew.

"Hey Mack, do you ever listen to my Mama and Daddy on the radio? They got a radio program, comes on every Sunday morning at 6:00. *Chapel of the Chimes*, brought to you by Williams Thomas Funeral Home. You ever hear it?"

Mack munched on his sandwich and shook his head.

"Well, you ought to listen sometime. It's a good program. My daddy plays the organ and sings. My mama reads her poetry. They're good people. Everybody says so."

When Mack and I finished our lunch, my mama came out and took our plates, my glass and Mack's cup. She washed them; then she put Mack's cup way up high, on top of the refrigerator like a fragile piece of art. I would be grown before I learned that Mack's cup was not special in Mama's mind, not in the way I thought it was special. Mack's cup was put way up high and out of the way so no one would accidentally drink after a black man.

I told that story to the playwriting group and, as we left the building, David Prete hurried to catch up with me. "Hey, I liked your story today. If you're serious about writing your stuff, I'd like to work with you." David, a writer, actor and director, was in Memphis for a year while his girlfriend, Rebecca Skloot, finished writing her book, *"The Immortal Life of Henrietta Lacks."*

And so it was that David and I began meeting for daily writing sessions. We met at Republic Coffee Shop where I wrote on a legal pad and David hammered out pages on his laptop. I told David about my childhood, and we picked out characters and memories that needed to be included in a one-woman play. After several months of writing and editing, we were ready to put the play on its feet. We started meeting in the theater lab at the University of Memphis and David had me show him how my father walked and talked. He had me show him gestures that would identify my mother as a character. We made decisions about the set for the show as we wrote dialogue for the fourteen characters I would portray on stage. The set became a wooden swing set, fourteen feet long and five feet wide. It had a ladder on one end, a tire hanging on a rope next to the ladder and a wooden swing on two ropes at the other end. A wooden bench sat downstage right, and a metal bucket was placed center stage. David was director of the show we called, *For Goodness Sake*.

I performed before sold-out houses in September of 2010. The audience response was powerful. David hugged me backstage after the premiere performance and cried as he said, "We did a good thing! We did a good thing!"

I took the performance to Milwaukee where I performed for a progressive Catholic Conference. I took the show to California where I performed for a United Church of Christ congregation in Modesto. And I took the show to Montpelier, Vermont where I performed for the Unitarian Church and in the Hyde Park Opera House. Following each performance, I sat down on the stage and invited the audience to engage in conversation with me. People wanted to share their own experiences of racism and injustice. The conversations helped me see the power of storytelling. Sharing my story of the black boy in the field helped me and helped audience members heal from past violence and trauma.

I wrote a second play, *Skin and Bones*, about my experiences of childhood sexual abuse and my eating disorder. Alice Berry directed that performance, and we staged the show at Theatre South in Memphis in September of 2013. Again, I sat on the stage following each performance and invited the audience to talk about their own experiences with food and body image. Healing occurred.

I felt so fortunate to be able to write my stories and to share them with open-hearted audiences. Because Anna supported me, I had the time to write, rehearse and produce the two plays. Because I had theater friends in Memphis, I was given the space and feedback I needed to stage the performances and to attract audiences. Because my work caught the attention of local newspapers, radio hosts and television programs, the word got out that my work was valuable and worth seeing. I was fortunate, and I recognized that.

My good fortune inspired me to wonder about people who don't get a chance to share their stories, people who are silenced by circumstances and systems. I considered nursing home patients, and I went into nursing homes where I listened to the life stories of residents, met with family members, wrote a brief biography, and framed it along with a photograph that I hung over the patient's bed. It gave the nursing staff a different perspective on the person they were bathing, helping to the toilet and wheeling to the dining room. That person had not always been so frail and needy. They had lived a whole life and each one of them had contributed to the life of others in some way. I loved making those nursing home stories come to light.

I went into the Shelby County Jail and asked if I could sit in a circle with twelve women who were incarcerated there.

I met with the circle on Monday and Thursday evenings after dinner. On the first night I gave each woman a pen, a legal pad, and copies of three books: *I Know Why the Caged Bird Sings* by Maya Angelou, *The Diary of Ann Frank* and *Their Eyes Were Watching God* by Zora Neale Hurston. We read the books and discussed them. I gave the women large sheets of heavy art paper along with crayons and markers. They created life-maps and shared them in class, telling their life's journey and showing us where they hoped to go from where they were.

We met for three months, thirty-two sessions. At the end of those sessions, I took the stories the women had shared, and I wrote a script based on those stories. Then I recruited professional actors to perform. I recruited musicians to play, a director and a stage manager. We performed *Prison Stories* on Thursday night inside the prison for the prison staff and all the women who were incarcerated there. On Friday and Saturday nights we performed in a local theater for public audiences. My goal for the women involved in the storytelling circle was for them to find a way to be free from whatever was holding them down, to find some degree of healing from past violence and trauma. My goal for the public audience was that they might realize women who are incarcerated are much more than whatever it was that happened to land them in jail. I facilitated seven semesters of Prison Stories and it is the best work I have ever done. I sometimes hear from women who participated in the project, and they tell me how much it meant to them, to share their story and to discover their own truths. Trust happened in the circles.

The work I was doing caught the attention of Craig Leake, a filmmaker, who was teaching at the University of Memphis. He asked if he could bring a film crew inside the prison and film a semester of Prison Stories. I was sure I could not get permission for that. Cell phones were not allowed inside the prison; I was certain the administration would veto an entire film crew with lights, cameras and microphones.

And I might have been denied the chance to bring Craig and his class of film students inside with me. But something happened, something I could not have predicted or planned. It all began on a cold November morning. I looked out our kitchen door and saw that the water in the bird bath was frozen. I shivered and called to Anna, "You're going to need more than a sweater when you go out this morning." Just then my phone rang. It was a friend, Brad Wallace, who volunteered at Manna House, a safe place for people who live without a permanent address, a place to get warm clothes, a shower, coffee and friendly conversation. Brad was calling me to share his anger.

"How long is this going to go on?" he asked. "When we got here this morning, we were met by a young woman nearly frozen at the door. She was released from the county jail last night, let out of the bus at the corner of Adams and Danny Thomas. She was wearing one of those paper suits and flip-flops. I honestly do not know how she survived the night. We got her in here and found some clothes to fit her. But what I want to know is how we can stop the county prison system from doing this. It's altogether inhumane."

I agreed and I called the warden of the prison who had the county public relations man, Steve Renfroe, contact me. Steve was upbeat and confident as he said, "The jail wouldn't release an inmate in a paper suit, certainly not on a night like we had last night."

"But the woman *was* released in a paper suit," I stated firmly.

"Well, if you could find that woman and she could testify to that, I might concede the point."

"I'll find her," I promised. I knew from past experiences and from the stories shared by women in the system that the paper suits were commonly given to women and men who had no belongings to retrieve and no one, family or friends, to bring clothes and pick them up. The blue jump suits are made of the same material as sturdy paper towels. They zip up the front.

214

I drove over to Manna House and learned that the woman had left without giving any personal information. No one knew her name or where she had gone. "She was young, about twenty-two, and she seemed to be new to the street," Brad was able to share that much information. He described her as thin, about five feet and six inches tall, with long brown hair. I took that information to The Hospitality Hub, an office where people who have no permanent address can have their mail delivered, store things in a locker, get coffee and get connected to resources in the city. My friend, Kelcey Johnson, had seen her and her name was Mandy. She had been given information about the Missionaries of Charity on Seventh Street. And Kelcey believed I could find Mandy there. I did. I found Mandy at the shelter and I told her that I was looking for her to ask if she had been released the previous day wearing nothing but a paper suit. She confirmed and I called Steve on my phone. "I've found Mandy, and she wants to tell you what she was wearing last night when she was released."

Steve had the warden contact me. "Elaine, this is Warden Thompson. And I owe you an apology. I'd like to meet with you at whatever place you choose. I need to talk with you if you would be so kind as to give me a chance to properly apologize."

I was surprised and delighted to invite the warden to meet with me at Theatre South, the place where I staged my one-woman shows and the Prison Stories performances. The warden met me there. He put his hat in his hands, and I showed him around the theater. We sat down and he said, "I want you to know that, when I took this job, I became aware of those paper suits and I, like you, was appalled by the practice of turning men and women loose on the street wearing nothing but paper. I vowed to myself that I would get rid of those paper suits. I really intended to do that. But one thing and then another has taken priority in my job, and I confess I let that vow slide to the bottom of my to-do list. I'm not proud of that. I am grateful to you for bringing it back to my attention. I'll see to it we get rid of those things."

"Thank you. I really appreciate that." The warden and I talked about the county jail. I had a chance to tell him about the program I facilitated, and he listened carefully as I shared several stories the women had shared with me.

"Is there anything else I can do for you?" the tall black man stood and put his hat on his head.

I gulped. "Yes, as a matter of fact there is a favor, I'd like to ask of you. There's a filmmaker in town who has asked to make a documentary of the work I do in your jail. His name is Craig Leake and he has asked if he can bring a film crew into the jail over the next three months, filming my next series of classes and the final performances."

"Consider it done. I'll spread the word that I've given you permission to do that. Sounds like a good thing. I look forward to seeing the film when it's finished."

The film was titled *Inside Story*, a twenty-seven-minute documentary. The film was shown on the local PBS station. It won a Regional Emmy Award in 2015. Anna and I had dinner with Craig and his wife on the evening of the awards ceremony. Craig, who had been awarded Emmy's in the past, thought that our film, although it was nominated for an award, would not be the winner. "I've seen the competition," he explained, "and we're just fortunate to be nominated." But he was wrong. Our film won and Craig was as pleased and surprised as I was. The Emmy was mailed to Craig since we hadn't made the trip to Nashville for the award ceremony. The award sits in his office beside his other Emmy's.

I show the film to youth groups who come through Memphis on Freedom Journeys, visiting the National Civil Rights Museum and learning about the history of slave trade in downtown Memphis. And I show the film to senior citizens in my creative writing classes, showing them the power of personal storytelling. Everyone has a story to share, every story is valuable, and nobody deserves to be silenced.

# Black Lives Matter

June 26 of 2015, the Supreme Court of the United States ruled that gay and lesbian couples could be married in their own states. I performed a wedding for our friends, Laura Harris and Nancy Wiers, on the lawn of the courthouse that day. It was a day of great celebration and joy. Anna and I talked about getting married. We had been together for almost sixteen years; we were happy with our relationship. But, if we married, I could be insured under Anna's health insurance. That factor was a major influence in our decision to be legally married.

On November 21, 2015, we were married by our friend, Rev. Dr. Mary Lin Hudson, in a beautiful room that had previously been a Masonic lodge. Our cake was made by our friend, Carrie Brooks. And photographs were taken by our friend, Thomas Greene. A string trio played as we walked to the front to exchange our vows. Jennifer played recorded music during the reception that followed the ceremony. We danced and ate together. It was a beautiful day. We felt the love and happiness of all our friends and family.

In July 2016, *Black Lives Matter* supporters in Memphis started messaging each other that they had had enough. Enough injustice and enough loss of life. As texts were sent to families and friends, people began to gather downtown. The numbers increased as the group marched through town and up the ramp onto the I-40 bridge that crosses the Mississippi River, connecting Tennessee and Arkansas.

Several hundred protesters blocked traffic on the bridge for over four hours that Sunday night. The Memphis police chief, a black man, joined the group and engaged the group leaders in conversation. The police SWAT team showed up prepared for trouble, but the protest ended peacefully. No one was injured, and no property was destroyed.

The following week, local *Black Lives Matter* leaders called Memphis' clergy together for two days of conversation, panel discussions, and guest speakers. I was serving as interim pastor at Shady Grove Presbyterian Church at the time and joined my colleagues at St. Mary's Episcopal Cathedral.

Rev. Floridia Jackson spoke directly to the white clergy, "You liberal white preachers are willing to talk the good talk from the safety of your own liberal pulpits. But you don't come out of your houses when black people take over the street. You see a crowd of us, and you think *dangerous*. You need to step out of your comfort zone! You need to get out of your house and into the street. You need to stand with us."

When I had been watching the bridge takeover on TV from the safety of my own home with my wife at my side, I remember thinking, "That is a recipe for disaster! Somebody is going to get shot or thrown over the bridge railing." I had been guilty of exactly what Floridia insisted was true of liberal white people.

I had recognized faces in the crowd and may have breathed a prayer for the protesters, but I am not sure I did even that much. I do know that I was glad to feel safe with my concern. That day at the cathedral, as Rev. Jackson spoke, I felt that she was speaking to me, and I resolved to step out of my comfort zone. The next time I heard about a protest, I would show up.

I didn't have to wait long. On August 16, Keedran Franklin, a leader of *Memphis' Coalition of Concerned Citizens*, announced plans for a protest at Graceland during the annual candlelight vigil marking Elvis Presley's death. The protest was named *Operation Blue Suede Shoes* and was intended to highlight the disparities in economic systems for whites and blacks in Memphis. In announcing the event, Franklin told the press, "What works for a few doesn't work for the many."

At five that evening I drove south on Elvis Presley Boulevard, with no idea what I might do or how long I might stay, but I was determined to show up. Seeing a sea of blue lights ahead of me, I parked the car and walked several blocks toward Graceland. Six police cars were parked, bumper to bumper, blocking traffic on the boulevard. A white tank loomed behind the line of cars. As I passed Graceland's parking lot, I spotted a black SUV—a police vehicle—just as a SWAT team member opened the back of the vehicle, revealing several boxes labeled AMMUNITION.

I wondered what the police expected to happen that evening and how much danger I was willing to face. I expected to see familiar faces in front of Graceland, but there were no protest signs and no one I knew.

I scanned the television news crews and walked up to the Channel 3/WREG camera man. "Have you seen any protesters? Do you know where they are?"

"They must have changed their minds about coming," he said.

Not convinced, I continued to the south end of Graceland's property. There I saw another row of police cars blocking traffic. I also recognized three men who were standing inside a small, fenced area that resembled a corral.

I laughed. "What are you guys doing inside there?" It looked like a joke.

"This is where the police say we can hold our protest," one said.

I was incredulous. The corral was far from Graceland's gates where tourists would see us and perhaps learn something about racial disparities in Memphis. I walked around to the opening and joined them.

We took pictures of ourselves as others joined our group. By six o'clock, the corral was too small to hold the protesters. There were about seventy of us. People began to press against the human barrier of police, who were standing shoulder to shoulder across the four lanes of the boulevard. A tank rolled toward us as the police announced, "Move out of the street!"

Wanting to march to the gates of Presley's mansion, protesters pressed even harder against the police, but to no avail. A few people were injured in scuffles with the police. White people who appeared to be Elvis Presley fans were cordially allowed to pass the police line, but when I tried to break through, the officer recognized me and said, "Stand back." No black people were allowed beyond the police barrier. And neither was I.

"Are you seeing this?" I asked a new friend, Pearl Walker, an African American woman who owned a shop just south of Graceland.

Pearl and her son held candles. She and her son had been forcibly restrained. They had planned to attend the vigil at Elvis's grave, but the police were not allowing them or other black fans to get close to the gates.

At 7:00, I was hungry. The group was not making progress toward the gate of Graceland.

I turned to Pearl, "I'm going home." I pointed north toward my car, beyond where the police were allowing us to go.

"Good luck," Pearl responded with a wry grin.

I might not have tried it, had I been less hungry. But I headed for the fence, believing my chances of getting back to my car were greater if I climbed over the fence on the side away from the human police line. I ran and leaped up to the top of the fence and threw one leg over. I could feel my heart pounding. I expected a shout from the officers, and my plan was to ignore them and run. But there was no shouting and, although I was in clear sight of police, no one tried to stop me, a 65-year-old white woman with graying hair.

A Graceland security guard who was passing by extended his hand. "You want some help there, ma'am?"

I walked past Graceland and the police at the north end of the property. Inside my car, I took a deep breath, then posted pictures on Facebook, writing, "Wow! Blatant racism before my very eyes. The police are not allowing anyone who is black to get near the gates of Graceland. But white people like me are allowed to go wherever they want, even if they climb over the police barricade!"

When I got home, I told my wife about the experience. We sat on the couch in our living room just as a bright light flashed outside our front window. A police car was outside; its search light aimed at our house. The squad car sat in front of our house for several minutes before moving on.

The next morning, I received a call from the assistant to State Senator Lee Harris. "The senator will hold a press conference tomorrow afternoon at Graceland, accusing the city and the police department of racial discrimination. We saw your Facebook post and he would like for you to tell the media about your experience last night. He's also invited Pearl Walker to share her story." I agreed to go.

It was pouring rain as we stood on the corner of Elvis Presley Boulevard and Craft Road surrounded by television cameras and huge umbrellas. The senator spoke eloquently about fairness, freedom, and equal rights under the law. Then Pearl and I spoke, telling our stories.

In the ensuing months I participated in other protest events, but none as intense as the Graceland experience. One night, more than a year later, in February 2017, after attending a performance at Germantown Performing Arts Center, thirty messages popped up on my phone, none of which made sense to me. Chris Davis, a writer for *The Memphis Flyer*, had posted: "What? Elaine Blanchard is a security threat to the City of Memphis? Oh, this will be Mayor Strickland's finest hour!"

Chris sent me a screenshot of a list of eighty-one names that had been shown on the evening news, my name included. The list included pastors, social justice advocates, community organizers, former city employees, and Mary Stewart, the mother of 19-year-old Darrius Stewart, who had been shot and killed by a Memphis police officer in 2015. I learned that I, along with everyone else on the list, would be required to have a police escort if we entered city hall. I laughed out loud.

# BLANCHARD VS CITY OF MEMPHIS

My new employer at a nonprofit organization, *Thistle and Bee*, was not laughing when she called me the next morning. The organization I worked for needed the support and goodwill of city officials and the police department. We were planning a fundraising breakfast to introduce our organization to the mayor, chief of police, and city council members, along with local philanthropists and business owners. We supported women on the street, helping them find safe and meaningful work.

"How are you?" she asked.

"I'm fine," I said.

"Well, I'm not. Frankly, your name being on that list is not good for our organization. We can't have our program director identified as an antagonist toward the very people we need to support us. Let's take this up again when I've had more time to think about it."

The conversation was brief and when it ended, I remained employed, but it was clear that my new position was threatened.

The next day she told me that I should lay low until we could get past the fundraising event. But it was not possible for me to keep a low profile. My name was in the local paper for several days as the *blacklist* story generated a buzz around town. Local television stations interviewed me. I joined others on the list in an event at city hall, protesting the fact that we had been identified as security threats without being informed that we were a danger to anyone and that we were singled out, not because of any threat we had posed, but because we had nonviolently protested racism and inequality in the city's economic systems.

When asked why he had signed the blacklist, Mayor Jim Strickland said he had signed without reading the names. Later he said he thought that activists on the list had taken part in a *die-in* on his private lawn, which was the reason their names were included. I had not been near his home, nor did I know where the mayor lived. Video footage of that event was easily available for anyone to see the small number of people who participated in the die-in, an event where protesters laid down on the ground in the mayor's yard, representing the lives of black citizens who had died at the hands of police violence. The video did not include me.

Attorney Bruce Kramer joined us at city hall. "The list may violate a federal court order issued in 1978 in response to a lawsuit litigated on behalf of the American Civil Liberties Union. The consent decree bans political surveillance following revelations the department spied on civil rights activists, war protesters, and other *radicals* for years."

A group of us gathered a few days later in Kramer's office, where he described how protesters of the Viet Nam War had had their rights violated by Memphis police in 1978. The city had gathered information through undercover surveillance and had used information to intimidate the protesters. After that, a consent decree was issued, barring the city and the police department from intimidating future nonviolent protesters. Bruce Kramer had represented the protesters and won the case against the City of Memphis.

I learned through our attorney's research that police had followed and intimidated persons in our group who had posted items about the recent protest on Facebook. The police department was using an app that searched social media for certain words and phrases. They had seen my Facebook post after the Graceland event.

Kramer had also discovered that a police officer had posed as a black social justice activist and had been accepted on the Facebook friends list of many of us. The police had also been sharing our names in joint intelligence briefs with major Memphis employers, including the U. S. military, the Department of Justice, Auto Zone, Fed Ex, and St Jude Children's Hospital.

On February 22, 2017, four of us were named as plaintiffs in a suit against the City of Memphis for violating our First Amendment Rights and for contradicting the 1978 consent decree. Mediation events were held, involving the plaintiffs and City of Memphis attorneys. The city claimed we were not eligible to bring suit because we had not been plaintiffs in the original case. As a result of that claim, Tennessee ACLU stepped in as a fifth plaintiff, having been a plaintiff in the original case.

Despite overwhelming evidence to the contrary, attorneys for the city believed they could win. They had every opportunity to negotiate with us and not go to court. Instead, on August 20, 2018, our case went to federal court (U.S. District Court Western District of Tennessee) for a bench trial with Judge Jon McCalla. The case is known as *Blanchard vs City of Memphis.*

I had never been to court as either plaintiff or witness, so the experience was educational at best and wearisome at worst. Witnesses were not allowed to sit in the courtroom. Rather, we were held in a small room out of earshot of others' testimony. On the first day of court, I had no idea I would need a way to pass hours in the witness waiting room. The following days I brought reading material, snacks, and drinks. When each of us was called to testify, we left the waiting room, told our stories, and only then were we allowed to sit in the courtroom and listen to the proceedings, which lasted four full days. The city filled the courtroom with high dollar attorneys and boxes and boxes of briefs.

Two months later, on October 26, 2018, the judge gave his ruling in favor of the plaintiffs. "The failure was one of training and inadequate direction over a sustained period of time," Judge McCalla wrote in a 39-page opinion.

Daniel Jackson from the Courthouse News Service reported that "a federal judge in Memphis ruled Friday that the city's failure to properly train members of its police department caused it to violate a 1978 agreement not to collect political intelligence on activists exercising their First Amendment rights."

The result was significant. The court imposed sanctions designed to ensure future compliance with the consent decree, including requirements that the Memphis police department revise their policy on political intelligence, train officers, establish a process for approving criminal investigations that may incidentally result in gathering political intelligence, establish written guidelines for the use of social media searches, maintain a list of all search terms used in social media collators, and submit the list to the court quarterly. The court also appointed an independent monitor to supervise the implementation of these sanctions.

The *Commercial Appeal* reported that "this important decision ensures that activists in Memphis can continue to fight the good fight without fear of unwarranted police surveillance."

Tennessee ACLU Executive Director Hedy Weinberg said, "The right to free speech is crucial to our ability to speak out against injustice and to hold the government accountable. Being able to truly engage in dialogue about important issues without the threat of intimidation is vital to our democracy."

Rev. Floridia Jackson's words and witness inspired me to step out of my comfort zone, and by doing so, I have learned so much. As a result of my commitment to simply show up, I saw that my white privilege could be put to good use in the fight against racism. I learned that I have the power to make a difference, to effect change in policy and practice. I am not a helpless bystander in the struggle for justice. Once I made a personal decision to get in the car and drive to Graceland, the rest of the story played out as if it were scripted.

# EPILOGUE

I have been the pastor at First Christian Church in Union City since October of 2018. I've been driving the distance for six years. The drive takes over two hours, from my home in Memphis, to the church. After church, I drive back again. I talk to God as I drive. It's quite a commute and well worth the effort. The congregation is helping to heal me from the wounds I've sustained through the years. And I am helping them to heal from past wounds and current fears. We are good for each other. I am seventy-two now and I want to conclude my career in ministry by being in love with what I do.

When I met with the search committee at First Christian Church, I made it clear that I am married to a woman, and I don't keep my marriage a secret, no more than heterosexual couples keep their marriages a secret. I told them I had lost my standing as an ordained minister. The three search committee members nodded their heads emphatically.

Having an un-ordained lesbian for their pastor was not going to be a problem. But after a story ran in the local newspaper, reporting that First Christian Church had a new pastor and she lived with her wife in Memphis, the phones blew up. "Are you that desperate?" people from more conservative churches asked. "Haven't you read Leviticus and Romans?" The chairperson of the search committee and his wife had to leave First Christian Church because their son threatened to isolate them from their grandchildren if they kept attending that church with its lesbian leader. And another couple had to leave because a daughter threatened estrangement. When the Obion County Ministerial Alliance read the article in the paper, the board members called an emergency meeting to change the bylaws of their organization, ensuring that no gay or lesbian person could belong to their alliance.

Union City is a small town, population of about 11,000. The town is surrounded by farmland, producing cotton, soybeans and corn mainly. The public schools are excellent, highly rated in the state for academics, band and sports. The teachers have roots and a deep concern for their students. It's an old town where once there were good jobs. Once there was a huge Good Year Tire Company, a large Tyson Chickens packing plant and a medical equipment manufacturing plant.

Those jobs have vanished and beginning job opportunities are fast food, Walmart and elder care. It's hard to get started in Union City so those who can move to a more prosperous city, do move. The young people have found other places to live, so my congregation is made up of senior citizens. We have a few young people, seven regulars, and a Sunday school class for them. We love our youngsters, and we have no idea whether they will be able or even willing to carry on the work of the church when the rest of us are gone. I don't think the reality of their burden has occurred to them; they just enjoy the present.

I am happy with my ministry among the folks at First Christian Church. I feel loved and I certainly love them. We have grown in number since I arrived, going from a regular attendance of twelve to an average attendance of twenty-four. We gained some excellent new members when the Methodists in town voted to leave the United Methodist denomination in favor of more conservative stances related to gender and homosexuality. More liberal people came over to First Christian and we are thrilled to have them. We are growing in more ways than numerically. Our spirits are expanding as we meet week after week and prayerfully sustain our faith.

I have written this memoir because I know I am not the only person to suffer abuse as a child, and I am not the only person to struggle with an eating disorder. I know other people have experienced struggles like mine. And it is for those people that I am telling my story. I want to be clear that hope is always available through trust in God. I trust that God is with me and has been with me through all of my experiences. And that includes the times when my shadow side took control, and I behaved in ways that were wrong. Even then, I was not abandoned. My God cries with me when I cry and rejoices with me when I am glad.

Since our grandson's birth, Doug and I have become friends again. He no longer gambles, and I no longer drink. With our addictions behind us and a grandchild to cherish, we enjoy one another again. All is forgiven.

Since Donald Trump was elected for a second time, I have joined other Memphians on the corner of Highland and Poplar, a busy intersection, to show signs of protest against the policies and actions of the current administration. We stand together from 4:30 to 5:30 every Monday afternoon. Most of us are senior citizens. We have time to protest regularly, and we have memories of protesting the Viet Nam War. We carry that history and the history of the Civil Rights Movement in our hearts. *The Mighty Souls Brass Band*, plays for us as we hold our signs and wave at passing traffic. I always carry my beautiful Pride flag, striped in diverse colors.

At the close of our hour-long protest, we gather together and sing "America, the Beautiful."

I love my life and the United States of America. I am privileged to be living in this nation as a healthy, white, well-educated woman. I am concerned about the direction things are taking; freedoms being removed and immigrants being treated inhumanely; our international relationships being treated like a game show. I am concerned about the disdain for diversity and dwindling respect for higher education and science. I am concerned about increasing numbers of acts of political violence. My grandson, Abram, deserves to grow up in a world where progress is being made, where racism is faced and fought, where church and state are kept separate, where the right to vote is considered sacred for every citizen, where we work together to take better care of our land, water and air so that generations to come can breathe easily. We are all in this together. I am determined to do all that I can to preserve the world's goodness for my daughter and grandson.

I would be remiss if I concluded this memoir without expressing my appreciation for the AA Central Gardens Group in Memphis. We meet weekly and lift each other up, sharing both joys and sorrows. It was a friend, Jack Richbourg, at Central Gardens Group who told me about Rip Coleman and Bohannon Hall Press. One thing I can do to help right what is wrong in the world is to stay sober. My recovery and my recovery friends are precious to me.

I've never learned the name of that black boy in the field in 1956. I don't know who he is or where he might be. I know that I am genuinely sorry for my part in the injuries that he and his family suffered. I know that good friends and trusted counselors have enabled my healing from the violence and trauma of that day so long ago. I hope the boy became a man and that he, too, has found support and compassion for what he endured. I continue to fight for racial justice because I remember that boy, his face and his feet. I remember that he was drooling, and the drool caught the sunlight and glistened. I remember knowing that it was wrong for him to be treated so cruelly. I couldn't speak up for him when I was four years old. But I can speak up now. My voice can be lifted for justice for every mother's son and daughter in honor of that black boy in the field.

www.ingramcontent.com/pod-product-compliance
Lightning Source LLC
Chambersburg PA
CBHW030919140626
46545CB00016B/1617